The Parent's Success Guide™ to Parenting

Edited by S. Blackthorn

WILEY

Wiley Publishing, Inc.

HQ
769
.P2756
2004

The Parent's Success Guide™ to Parenting

Published by
Wiley Publishing, Inc.
111 River St.
Hoboken, NJ 07030-5774
www.wiley.com

WILEY

About the Authors

Sandra Hardin Gookin, co-author of *Parenting For Dummies*, 2nd Edition, has a degree in speech communications from Oklahoma State University. Her communications background and experience in parenting methods have been the basis for her parenting theories. She is the mother of four boys.

Dan Gookin, co-author of *Parenting For Dummies*, 2nd Edition, has written more than 75 books about computers, and his works have been translated into 34 languages. Dan wrote the first *For Dummies* book (and many after that), so the light, humorous, and informative style of *For Dummies* books is Dan's style. He is the father of four boys.

Marlene Targ Brill, author of *Raising Smart Kids For Dummies*, is an early childhood specialist, special educator, and mother. Her background of multiple degrees in education, 13 years of teaching and training other teachers, and practical experience on the home front contribute to her parenting focus and practical suggestions.

Marion Peterson, MFT, co-author of *Single Parenting For Dummies*, has experienced divorce, single parenting, and blended family life firsthand. She has a master's degree in clinical psychology; is a Licensed Marriage, Family and Child Therapist; is certified in Scientific Marital Therapy; and has facilitated many groups, including those for Parents in Pain, single parents, and women in transition.

Diane Warner, co-author of *Single Parenting For Dummies*, writes for magazines, newspapers, and Web sites, and is the best-selling author of 21 books. She is also a professional speaker and has made appearances on national television and radio, including Discovery Channel, CNN, and Home & Garden TV.

Diane Stafford, co-author of *Potty Training For Dummies*, taught high-school journalism and English and then became a writer/editor, serving as editor-in-chief of many publications, including *Health & Fitness Magazine* and *Texas Woman Magazine*. She has won awards for health writing, and now edits and writes books.

Jennifer Shoquist, MD, co-author of *Potty Training For Dummies*, is a family-practice physician and serves as a health-issues resource for journalists. She completed her medical degree at the University of Texas Medical School at Houston, followed by family-practice residency at Memorial Southwest Hospital.

Sue Fox, author of *Etiquette For Dummies*, is the Founder and President of Etiquette Survival, Inc. (formerly The Workshoppe) and ESK Publishing Group (a California-based professional development and publishing company). She provides group training and private consultations to business professionals, corporations, children, and educational institutions. She is the mother of two sons.

Sandra Blackthorn has a degree in journalism from Indiana University and has been involved with *For Dummies* books since 1992, serving first as a project editor, senior editor, and editorial manager, and now as a freelance writer and consultant. She is the mother of two children.

Publisher's Acknowledgments

Some of the people who helped bring this book to market include the following:

Editor: Elizabeth Kuball

Acquisitions Editors: Holly Gastineau-Grimes, Joyce Pepple

Technical Editor: Wendy Koebel, MSW, CSW, ACSW

Cover Photo: ©Getty Images

Table of Contents

Table of Contents

☺ ☺ ☹ ☺ ☺ ☹ ☺ ☺ ☹ ☺ ☺ ☹ ☺ ☺ ☹ ☺ ☺ ☹ ☺

Table of Contents

Part 1

Parenting Basics

T he Egyptians knew that to make the whole pyramid concept work, they had to start with a strong, solid base. This base had to be all encompassing and broad enough to handle the weight of everything that went on top of it. Making a good pyramid took a long time. Many attempts at building pyramids failed, but those aren't the structures that you see in pictures or get to tour.

This part serves as a solid base for building a parenting pyramid. The following four chapters provide you with information and guidelines that can help you construct the sturdy foundation upon which you can build a great relationship with your kids. As was true of the original pyramids, you'll run into stumbling blocks when you work on your parenting skills. But if you have a strong foundation, your kids can pile all kinds of stuff on you and you'll handle it just fine.

Chapter 1

Primary Parenting Principles

Welcome to The Parenting Game! Your goal is to raise children who turn into well-adjusted adults, but you can't play the game without knowing the primary parenting principles. That's what this chapter shows you.

Know up front that no parent is perfect, so all you can do is your level best. If your kids grow up to be happy, wholesome, and productive adults — people who are valued in the community — and you wind up having a wonderful relationship with them, then you've won the game.

First Things First: Using This Book

This book is part of a series called *The Parent's Success Guide.* Its main purpose is to help you, a busy, multitasking mom (or dad!), make some positive changes in your life as a parent — in a minimum amount of time.

Brought to you by the makers of the world-famous *For Dummies* series, this book provides straightforward advice, hands-on information, and helpful, practical tips — all of it on, about, and for being a smart parent. And this book does so with warmth, encouragement, and gentleness — as a trusted friend would do.

This book isn't meant to be read from front to back, so you don't have to read the entire book to understand what's going on. Just go to the chapter or section that interests you. And although age-specific information is included for toddlers, preschoolers, school-age children, and teenagers, this book is more of a reference for parents of children of all ages. Keep an eye out for text in *italics*, which indicates a new term and a nearby definition — no need to spend time hunting through a glossary.

☺ ☺ ⊗ ☺ ☺ ☹ ☺ ☺ ☹ ☺ ☺ ☹ ☺ ☺ ⊗ ☺ ☺ ☺ ☹ ⊗ ☺

While reading this book, you'll see these icons sprinkled here and there:

 This icon points out advice that saves time, requires less effort, achieves a quick result, or helps make a task easier.

 This icon signifies information that's important to keep in mind.

 This icon alerts you to areas of caution or danger — negative information you need to be aware of.

If you'd like more comprehensive information about a particular subject covered in this book, you may want to pick up a copy of the classic *For Dummies* book covering the same topic. This book consists primarily of text compiled from

✿ *Parenting For Dummies,* 2nd Edition

✿ *Raising Smart Kids For Dummies*

✿ *Single Parenting For Dummies*

✿ *Etiquette For Dummies*

✿ *Potty Training For Dummies*

The Duties and Responsibilities of a Parent

Your job as a parent consists of several duties and responsibilities to your kids:

✿ You communicate effectively with them — expressing your specific ideas, wants, and desires — and teach them to do the same with you.

✿ You set fair and reasonable rules for them, never go back on or change those rules, and practice following through (meaning you always stick to your original word).

✿ You manage their behavior by keeping them busy and occupied most of the time, because idle hands get into trouble. You also give them time to relax and use their imagination in play, because scheduling every second of their lives can lead to an inability to do anything on their own. And all the while, you give them plenty of praise and attention as well as find the patience to deal with them in a calm and relaxed way.

- You keep them healthy by making sure that they get proper nutrition and sleep.
- You educate them with what you remember of your book learning and common sense.
- You guide them — physically, socially, and emotionally — through the good times as well as the tough times.
- You take care of them when they get sick, and you do your best to keep them safe and out of harm's way.
- You love them — unconditionally.

The Roles a Parent Must Play

One thing you need to understand is that, as a parent, you must take on some new and important roles — that of role model, teacher, listener, and friend who's still the parent. You can still be yourself, but parenting requires you to understand that regardless of whether you want to accept these new roles, they're yours. And it's for you and your kids' benefit that you play them well.

The positive role model

A *role model* is someone you look up to and try to be like. Maybe it's that woman down the street who raised five kids all to become doctors. Maybe it's a fictional character, like Batman. Or maybe it's your own mother or father. Whoever, it's someone you want to be like, someone who is well liked.

Being a positive role model is important because your children look to you as an example of how to behave. Your actions and behavior play a significant role as your child's personality develops. Regardless of what habits you have and actions you take, you can rest assured that your child is watching your every move and gathering that *that's* the behavior to imitate. What you do has a direct impact — positive or negative.

Know that you can be a role model in ways that you don't even realize. How you handle stress, how you communicate, and how you reassure your children are important aspects of being a positive role model.

A *good role model* isn't necessarily someone who is perfect in every way. If you can walk on water, that's great. Otherwise, try doing the things that you know are right. You'll no doubt get upset sometimes. That happens. The important part is to apologize later or explain to your kids why you got upset. It's healthy for kids to know that their parents get upset. Everyone does. *How* you handle being upset is what's important.

On the other hand, a *bad role model* doesn't necessarily mean a bad person. Bad role models typically are workaholics, alcoholics, drug users, negative people, or people who put material things ahead of their families.

The rewards of being a good role model are great. You'll raise children who grow up to be people others want to be friends with. They'll contribute to their communities and generally be all-around great people. And that's a great gift to society.

The ever-present teacher

Everything you do and say is absorbed by your child's brain. This happens whether you want it to or not, so welcome to your second role as parent — that of *teacher.* From the time your children are born, they watch your actions and behaviors and learn from them. Your children discover things when you talk to them and do things with them. You'll teach them how to respond to spilled milk, how to react to a joke, what to do when they fall down — and all the other things we deal with in life.

If you're calm, relaxed, and don't overreact to broken dishes and other such events, your children are likely to be calm and relaxed. On the other hand, if you're nervous and tense, your children are likely to be nervous and tense.

As a parent/teacher, you have two general areas in which you need to spend time teaching your children:

❋ **Relationships:** You want to enable your children to be their own people, have their own ideas, and recognize and respect the fact that your and their ideas can be different. In addition, the strongest relationships that parents and children can have with other people are those in which both can come together, accepting and respecting that they are different and have different thoughts and ideas. Achieving this balance takes a considerable amount of work on a parent's part, because kids instinctively consider their way of thinking right and think that everyone else must think that way, too.

❋ **Education:** Whether your kids attend public or private schools or are schooled in your home, you need to help them with their homework and other educational needs. Take the time to explain how things work and let your children help you cook, clean, and grow some flowers. This is all part of education.

The good listener

Listening is probably one of the weakest and most underused skills that people have. Listening to, paying close attention to, and focusing on your children are the greatest gifts you can give to them.

A technique known as *mirroring* — in which you repeat back what your child (or partner, for that matter) says or summarize those same thoughts — is great to use when you and your child are talking. For example, when your child comes home from losing a soccer game and tells you how much she hates soccer, you might mirror back a response such as "So you hate soccer" and then follow up with "Tell me more about that" or "It sounds like you're really upset that you lost the game." Then be quiet and let your child talk. Mirroring not only clarifies what's being said but also keeps you on track with the conversation and serves as an acknowledgement for your child that you're actually paying attention. In addition, it helps teach your child to express her feelings in healthy ways. It's also a wonderful skill to use in conversations with your friends and other family members.

The friend who's still the parent

How can parents *befriend* their children and still function as parents? This question is tough to answer and a difficult issue to approach. You want to be friends with your children, spending time together, doing things together, paying attention to each other, and helping them grow up to be healthy, strong, independent people. Wanting to be your children's friend can be very tempting. But you don't want to cross the line and forget about being a parent. Granted, it's not always fun. Parents have to make rules and enforce them, which often makes kids very upset. Friends, on the other hand, get to do fun things and usually make each other happy.

When you feel tempted to be more of a friend than a parent, remember that, during the course of their lives, your kids will have lots of *different* friends, but *no one* can replace your role as a parent. So don't lose that role while trying to be your children's friend.

An excellent book for parents is *The Emotional Incest Syndrome, What to Do When a Parent's Love Rules Your Life,* by Dr. Patricia Love. The title may be a tad scary. But this book shows you what to avoid. "Too much of a friend" can be defined as a parent who shares confidential information with a child or makes the child think of himself and that parent as "best friends." Becoming too much of a friend leads a child to believe that he must help you take care of your needs instead of you enabling him to grow and take care of his own needs.

The friend-versus-parent conflict isn't all doom and gloom; good parents can and do make things fun, the way that a good friend does. But beware of bad but not-so-obvious habits that you don't want to develop, such as *invalidating* a child with a problem, which you probably learned from your parents. Examples include telling a child to stop whining because nothing really is wrong with him or telling him to get up because he isn't really hurt.

Being a good parent to your children also means accepting them for who they are, which typically is what a friend does. It isn't harping on or

☺ ☺ ☹ ☺ ☺ ☹ ☹ ☺ ☺ ☹ ☺ ☺ ☹ ☺ ☺ ☹ ☺ ☺ ☺ ☹ ☺

pointing out their weaknesses but rather helping them build up the things they're good at. By encouraging them, you not only prove that you're a good friend but also help them develop their self-confidence.

Think about your best friend. How did this person become your best friend? You probably just spent a lot of time together and had fun, and the next thing you knew, you were friends. The same thing can happen with your children. Raising kids isn't the time to be selfish with your time or energy. It's the time when you *make time* to be with and do things with your kids.

If your children are your friends, they're more likely to open up to you with their problems and concerns about school, peer pressure, or other things that bother them. Likewise, you'll be more approachable when your kids look to you not only as a parent but also a friend.

The Importance of Keeping Your Sense of Humor

If you're like many parents, you probably can't think of anything or anyone more entertaining than your children. They're funny. They're goofy. Perhaps that's why so many good books, movies, and even comic strips are based on children and the things they do.

Without being evil, children have an uncanny ability to push all your buttons. You really need to be able to laugh at the things that ordinarily would drive you up the wall. In other words, relax.

Anger is usually a parent's first reaction because what kids do is unexpected, and it's also usually the parent who has to clean it up. So what? Stop, take several deep breaths, look at that sweet face, and smile. Anger is wasted energy, and you want to spend that energy somewhere else.

Let your kids be kids. They goof up. They make messes. Accept that fact and never assume they're doing something "just to get you." Part of the joy of being a parent is sitting back and watching your kids do all the goofy things your parents accused you of doing when you were a kid.

Concern for your children is good. But don't be so protective of your children that you forget how fun kids can be. Laughing is great. It makes you feel good, it relieves stress, and it makes life a lot more fun.

Chapter 2

From the Beginning, Communication Is Key

Good communication skills are the foundation for building a great relationship with your kids. However, so many different elements get thrown in the way that listening and communicating aren't always easy or effective.

This chapter covers things you can do to improve communication with your kids and provides some ideas about how to teach your kids to be good communicators.

Talking Effectively

If you have something to say and you want to be heard, you need to do the following:

❋ **Physically get down to your children's level.** If you can't squat, pick them up and put them on your lap. Look them right in the eye (and encourage them to look *you* in the eye).

❋ **Use simple words.** Getting your point across is easier when your kids know what you're talking about. Don't try to impress your children with your fabulous expanded vocabulary. Use words that your kids understand. If you don't think they understand, ask them to explain what you've just said. If they're missing your meaning, explain it to them in another way or define the word that's throwing them off.

☺ ☺ ☹ ☺ ☺ ☹ ☺ ☺ ☹ ☺ ☺ ☹ ☺ ☺ ☹ ☺ ☺ ☺ ☹ ☺

❀ **Get to the point.** Your kids understand you a lot better when you're specific and when you get right to the point, so don't be vague, don't babble or ramble, don't go into long explanations, and say exactly what you mean.

❀ **Don't yell.** When you yell at your kids, your message won't get across. They're not listening to a thing you're saying. All they're doing is sitting there teary-eyed and upset because you're yelling, or they're getting angry themselves. Your point is lost. Whenever you reach the point where you're about to yell, stop and leave the room. Get your composure back and approach the situation again. Speak calmly and slowly, and say what you have to say.

Remember: You're trying to be a role model and teacher. Yelling isn't a trait that you want to pass on to your kids. In fact, it comes back to haunt you as your kids grow older and their hormones get all stirred up. After all, when you yell, you're only teaching them to yell.

Avoiding problems caused by a lack of communication

You can reduce outbursts in grocery stores and other temper tantrums by explaining to your kids what you expect of them. Kids like to know what's going on just as much as you do; they like being prepared and informed. Here are some pointers for avoiding tantrums:

❀ Before whisking your children out of the house, give them time to prepare whatever things they need (tucking Barbie back in her Barbie Dream House before leaving or searching for a toy to bring along, for example).

❀ Look your children in the eye when you get to where you're going, making sure that you have their attention, and then tell them what your expectations are and why you expect this behavior.

❀ Never assume your kids know what you want; when you stop talking and start assuming, you get into trouble.

Be sure to plan wisely before putting your kids in an environment that's going to be difficult for them. Don't expect a 2-year-old to sit quietly in a theatre, at a wedding, or in an upscale restaurant. And remember that scolding a child for being a child when he's in an environment that he shouldn't be in to begin with is unfair.

In addition, know that advance planning works only when you don't give in to whining and change your mind about the rules. If you set rules but don't stick to them, you're in serious trouble. Your kids will always push you, whine, and throw fits whenever you go back on your word.

Teaching Basic Communication Skills

Communication skills must be taught, and communication — like everything else — has rules:

❀ **Use correct English.** If you ever expect your kids to speak properly, you must speak properly yourself. When you speak baby talk, your kids assume that's the way adults talk, too. If you call a blanket a blankey, for example, your children will call it that, which is neat for a while, but when you see a 5-year-old walking around calling a blanket a blankey, it isn't cute anymore. Teaching your kids to talk one way only to change it later isn't fair. English is hard enough; don't make it any harder.

❀ **Look children in the eye.** Do so from the moment they're born. Looking people in the eye establishes a sense of confidence and trust. And when there's eye-to-eye contact, everyone is paying attention.

❀ **Speak slowly and clearly.** Your kids will talk much like you do. Teach them to speak well by speaking slowly and clearly yourself and by telling them to slow down when they're overexcited and talking too fast. Don't make it sound like you're scolding them. Just tell them that you can understand better when they slow down.

❀ **Let children express themselves.** Having your kids express themselves is a wonderful way to teach them to communicate. When people express happiness, anger, disappointment, confusion, whatever, they must formulate their thoughts and then try to say what they feel. Encourage your kids to tell you how they feel. When you start training them how to open up to you, communicating their fears and frustrations will be easier by the time they go to school. That's when many of their feelings will pop up and need to be discussed.

❀ **Set an example.** The best way to teach anyone is by example, which means that you must follow the same rules you set for your kids. Be a good listener, don't interrupt, don't finish their sentences for them, and ask for more information to encourage conversation. In addition, resist the urge to hurry them up when they're telling a story. And no cursing, sarcasm, yelling, arguing, or lying, either.

❀ **Allow disagreements.** If your children disagree with you, it doesn't have to mean they're arguing, which is how many parents interpret disagreements. It just means they have a different opinion, which is good. When you encourage your kids to express their differing points of view by saying, "Tell me more about what you think," you're helping your kids explain their feelings, encouraging discussions, allowing your kids to be heard, and teaching fairness.

☺ ☺ ☻ ☺ ☺ ☻ ☺ ☺ ☺ ☻ ☺ ☺ ☻ ☺ ☺ ☻ ☺ ☺ ☺ ☺ ☻ ☺

✹ **Listen rather than just hear.** Listening is different from hearing. Hearing means that the noise is hitting your eardrum. You can be hearing what your children are saying, but you may not be listening. Listening means that you understand what they're saying, or even what they're not saying but really meaning. Being a good listener means not interrupting your children and not finishing their sentences for them, and it also means practicing *mirroring skills* in which you repeat back what your children say or summarize those same thoughts. Mirroring keeps you involved in the conversation, lets your children know that you're paying attention, and ensures that what you heard is what your children meant to say.

Remember: The most important part of communicating is being a good listener. Communication can't work both ways when you're doing all the talking and none of the listening.

Answering Awkward Questions

Your goal as a good parent is to be someone who communicates well and someone your children can approach. You want your children to be comfortable enough to ask you complicated or awkward questions.

You can answer awkward questions effectively by following these rules:

✹ **Rephrase the question — also known as *mirroring.*** Make sure that you understand exactly what your child is asking. The more you understand, the easier it is for you to answer. For example, when your child asks, "Why does Uncle Richard like to wear Aunt Robin's dresses?" you can say, "You want to know *why* Uncle Richard likes to wear Aunt Robin's dresses?"

✹ **Keep your responses simple.** Your children don't always want a textbook answer. If your child asks, "Where do babies come from?" you can say something simple like, "From mommies." When you answer your child's question and she skips off happily, you answered as much as she needed to know at that time. If she continues asking for more information, you may have to go into more detail and drag out the visual aids.

✹ **Try responding as quickly as possible.** If you're unable to answer at the time your child asks a question, follow up later. You don't want your child to feel that you're unwilling to answer his questions. If your child asks, "What's sex?" you can say, "Well, honey, sex is an interesting topic. How about we sit down after dinner and talk about it?"

✹ **Be observant.** If your child seems bothered by something or asks only vague questions (but never wants to go into detail), sit down and talk. Maybe something is bothering her that she's having problems talking about, or perhaps she's confused about something and doesn't quite know what to ask. For example, if your child asks, "Daddy, do you *love* me?" you respond with, "Yes, I love you. Why do you ask?"

Communicating with Stickers and Notes

Tired of telling your kids *every* morning to make their beds and brush their teeth? As a parent, you'd think they'd finally understand that they have to do this stuff every morning regardless of whether you've told them to. Maybe it's time to change the way you're telling them.

A good way to get kids to do things they don't like to do is to make those tasks as fun as possible. Tell your kids what you want them to do with notes (like the one shown in Figure 2-1) or charts and stickers (see Table 2-1).

Figure 2-1: You can communicate effectively and praise your kids through notes.

For example, make a chart listing your kids' daily chores. After they've done their chores, let them put a sticker beside each chore that they've finished. Tell them that if the chart is completed by a certain time (one that you set), they can do something special, like watch a favorite video. If they don't complete their chart, don't let them do whatever you've set as the special reward. Be consistent and don't give in to whining or big Bambi eyes filled with tears. This strategy works only when your kids know that you're serious.

☺ ☺ ☹ ☺ ☺ ☹ ☺ ☺ ☹ ☺ ☺ ☹ ☺ ☺ ☹ ☺ ☺ ☺ ☹ ☺

Table 2-1 Good Morning!

Chores	Mon	Tues	Wed	Thurs	Fri	Sat	Sun
Make your bed							
Put your pajamas away							
Brush your teeth							
Get your schoolwork done							
Feed the dog/cat							

Chapter **3**

Setting Boundaries, Being Consistent, and Following Through

In This Chapter

☺ Providing well-defined rules and guidelines about what will happen when your child breaks the rules

☺ Being consistent by not going back on or changing the rules and guidelines

☺ Following through by sticking to your word

The parenting game is played on a huge game board — but it has no squares! Your kids can run wherever they want. In fact, that's the rule they play by: Run amok. Your job as parent is to steer them and guide them (to set boundaries) as if little squares existed for them to move across.

But that's only part of your job. After you start steering and guiding them, you need to keep it up (be consistent) and stick to your words (follow through). Doing so requires hard work. Kids will power up the charm to get you to break. They'll smile. They'll cry. They'll throw tantrums like the pizza man tossing a pie. As long as you don't waver, though, the result will be well-behaved children. And, basically, anyone who meets your kids will be pretty grateful to you.

Setting Boundaries for Your Children

Setting boundaries means building walls for your children, and building walls for your children is important. These walls are mental barriers erected to keep your kids safe and you sane, and you build the walls by setting rules.

 As a parent, one of your jobs is to set boundaries — to provide well-defined rules as well as guidelines about what will happen when they are broken. Two subsequent jobs are being consistent with the rules and then following through with what happens when children break them (topics covered elsewhere in this chapter).

Here are a few of the customary limits parents set:

- **Where your children are allowed to play:** The play areas of very young children are limited, so decide carefully where those play areas are. You need to provide a safe environment for them and keep an eye on them, ensuring that they don't get hurt or wander off (see Chapter 16 for detailed safety advice). As your children grow older, you can start slowly expanding their territory, which depends largely on your house, yard, and neighborhood. If you live in the heart of New York City, your children's territory is different from that of children who live out in the countryside of Northern Idaho.

- **What kind of behavior is allowed with a big understanding that kids like to play like kids:** Kids don't play like adults (meaning orderly and quietly), so don't sabotage your children by putting them in an environment where they can't act the way they're supposed to. Fancy restaurants, weddings and funerals, live theatre, and movies are a few places where the environment is typically quiet. Children aren't quiet. That said, behavior that you need to keep an eye on is anything harmful to others, like hitting and throwing toys. The same goes for any behavior that is harmful to your children.

- **What your children can play with:** Everything your children see is a potential toy — buttons, coins, balloons, candy. You name it, and it has toy potential. Thing is, babies and toddlers have an annoying habit of putting everything in their mouths, regardless of the taste, because that's their way of exploring. Buttons, coins, balloons, and candy are things children typically choke on, so be critical in your decisions about what your children can play with. Similarly, you don't want to allow playing with the stereo one day and then get mad the next day when you catch a child resetting your treble and bass knobs.

Factors that encourage kids to thrive within the boundaries

When setting your rules and boundaries, think about the following key factors that encourage your child to thrive:

- **Devise rules that are fair.** Your 12-year-old shouldn't have the same bedtime as your toddler. Set guidelines that make sense for every member of the family.

- **Make sure rules are realistic.** Rules need to match your child's level of development and maturity. They must be simple and easy to understand, and they should always fit the situation they pertain to. Expecting a 10-year-old to keep his water glass off the marble table because it leaves a ring is fair and realistic. Expecting your son home from the prom at his usual eleven o'clock curfew is not.

✽ **Give reasons for rules when possible.** You don't always have the luxury of time to explain, and you don't want to go into long monologues. But providing a brief rationale for why a rule is important gives your child a chance to incorporate the rule into his own system of beliefs. He is empowered.

✽ **Bend rules for the rare but wonderful situations when they make sense.** Let your toddler stay up past eight o'clock to finish the story. Allow a pillow fight between siblings once in awhile, as long as light fixtures are glued to ceilings and tabletops. Allowing what's usually out of bounds gives your kids the message that you're not unreasonable. You appear less perfect and more approachable in their eyes when you put down your policing stick once in awhile.

Building walls around the TV, computer, and video games

Admit it. Sometimes, television, video games, and the computer function as a babysitter. Or they calm family beasts like a tranquilizer. No one says you have to pull the plug altogether, but limits are in order:

✽ **Put the family on a television diet.** Budget the time everyone – including you – watches TV. The American Academy of Pediatrics suggests limiting television viewing so that children under 2 years old never watch TV, children older than 2 and up to school-age watch in half-hour increments, and elementary-age kids watch at most two hours a day.

✽ **Agree on basic media rules and stick to them.** No media of any kind before bed. No television, video games, or Internet chats on school nights unless homework is finished or you agree beforehand on a brief after-school break. No television during meals together.

✽ **Set the rule that you *will* monitor your child's Internet use – and do it.** Supervise forays online, especially if your child is young and new to the Internet. Oversee which sites your child visits and what she downloads. Review your child's buddy list and address book. Check her profile and how she introduces herself. Delete people your child doesn't know. Help her clean out files and e-mail regularly.

✽ **Set ironclad rules about sharing personal information online.** Caution your child *never* to send family names (including her own) or an address, telephone number, school name, photo, or credit card information to strangers online.

Why kids always test boundaries, no matter what

Know up front that your kids will constantly push against the walls you build. They'll always test you, and they do so for two reasons:

❀ **They need to know where the walls are.** This knowledge makes them feel secure. Therefore, you must erect the walls and keep your kids within them if you want secure kids.

❀ **They need to grow.** Your children can't always have the rule not to play outside unsupervised. Eventually, they outgrow that rule — the same way they outgrow rules on naptimes and what they're allowed to play with.

Never interpret your kids' pushing against the walls as a reason for taking the walls down. Kids push, but they rely on your consistency. You must be consistent and keep those walls up for them to be secure, happy people (see the following section for details on being consistent). They get some sadistic pleasure in testing you, but they really do like for you to set their boundaries and have you enforce them.

Eventually, as your children grow older and more responsible, you'll move the walls outward (setting a later bedtime, for example) and enable them to do more things. But even then, they'll still push.

 Moving the walls outward is a delicate process that can cause stress with younger siblings. Changing an older sibling's bedtime schedule, for example, is best done in private so that other children don't moan and complain, "That's not fair!" (If your kids always know what's going on in each other's lives and you can't make private arrangements with your older child, try setting a firm rule that you can explain to the younger ones — for example, "When you're 13, you get to stay up an hour later, too.")

Being Consistent with the Rules

Being consistent means not going back on or changing the rules and guidelines you've established. It means not being wishy-washy with your kids. Even when the whining gets to you (and believe me, it *will*), you need to be firm.

When to be consistent

This is perhaps the toughest part of being a parent. When it comes to consistency, you must never yield. When your child crawls on the dining room table, you take him down *every time* he crawls back up. Don't pretend after a while that you don't see him. You may be tired of the game, but he has the energy of the Energizer Bunny and just keeps on going. Every time you take him off the table, you're being consistent.

A thousand or more examples of when you need to be consistent exist. Bedtimes need to be consistent, and so do meal times, homework times, rules about behavior, rules about how your household is set up (what furniture is okay to abuse and what isn't), and the list goes on.

 Being consistent sounds easy, but your kids have one up on you. They're cute; they cry; they beg; tiny arms reach up; tear-filled eyes beg for mercy; and lower lips protrude. But don't give in. Be strong. Be consistent. Your kids really want that from you. They need it. They want to know the guidelines, and they want you to be consistent about enforcing them.

"I'm too cute and precious for your feeble attempt at consistency"

The first several months of your children's lives you spend telling them how utterly cute they are. They're angels. They're cuddly. They're aware of this and store that knowledge for use in the future, when they can also use their countenances to pour on the charm. "Watch me light up Mommy like a Christmas tree." This is a learned behavior parents teach, and children can put it to good use.

When the time comes to be firm and consistent, think before you speak. You say what you mean. (It's the law, right?) But then comes the charmer. Out pops the lower lip. Eyes swell with tears. Emotional pain contorts the face. "How could you do such a thing to me when I live to love you?"

This is emotional warfare! It has a purpose, primarily to make you give in and part from being consistent. But this is the point where you can't give in. No matter what. You set out to be consistent, so stick with it. Don't change your mind.

The most amazing part of this emotional turmoil is that your kids don't really know they're doing this. The turmoil is all yours. Kids are just being true to themselves. They know what they want, and in their world, they truly think they deserve it. Kids are honest and brilliant and haven't been made to understand that crying because they didn't get a third cookie is unacceptable.

Bottom line? Your kids rely on you to be consistent. Don't let them down even though sticking to your guns can appear like just the opposite. If you give in, not only do you lose, but so does the charmer.

"Give me persistence, and I'll carve Mount Rushmore with a spoon"

You tell your child that if he chooses to throw food across the table then he won't get any dessert. He chooses poorly and throws the food anyway. Okay, no dessert. That's final. None.

Then the imp decides to clean his room or do some other chore you've been nagging him for and — lo and behold — a sweet-faced angel asks you for dessert. Don't waver! Your answer is still "No." Your child made the choice to throw the food (or whatever the choice was). It was his choice, so now the consequences of that choice must follow.

Persistence is the art of doing something again and again, maybe with subtle changes between repetitions, but nevertheless, again and again. Ever wonder why kids continue to ask, again and again, even after you say "No"? Because they perceive some remote chance that you'll change your mind. Why? Because, maybe, just maybe, at some time in the past, you changed your mind. That's the payoff of persistent effort.

You must be constant! Don't let persistence wear you thin. When you break down, everyone loses. You lose because the kids know how to get to you, and they lose because they need your constancy to keep them from turning into brats.

Give yourself more resolve to handle these situations wisely by thinking before you talk, by giving your child a choice ("Stop this behavior or this will happen"), and by reminding your child that he had a choice, but by not stopping, he chose, instead, to accept the punishment.

Your kids will continue testing you, but they won't spend as much time doing it when they realize that you don't go back on your word or succumb to whining and temper tantrums. After all, why bother when it doesn't work?

Two simple rules for you, the parent

As a parent, if you practice being consistent, consistency will be its own reward. Here are two simple rules to follow:

✸ **Think before you say something.** Being consistent is hard when you say something goofy or something you don't mean. As long as you've taken the time to consider your words, you need only to avoid the major weapon your child has to battle your consistency. And that is *persistence*. Children can be persistent with their whining and their demands. It's what they do. Just don't let it get to you so much that you back down. (For more on how good kids are at being persistent, check out the nearby sidebar called "Give me persistence, and I'll carve Mount Rushmore with a spoon.")

❋ **Make your rules realistic.** Don't set unrealistic expectations for your child. Being consistent is easier when you've set rules and guidelines that are simple and make sense. For example, don't put temptation, like an open electrical socket, in front of your children and expect them to follow the rule of not sticking a toy in it. They're naturally being themselves when wanting to stick things in holes. *Remember:* In addition, you can't be consistent on a rule that you'd like to set but that just doesn't jibe with having kids around. For example, you may want to establish the rule that all toys are kept in your children's rooms. But reality sets in, and you realize that such a rule is impossible to enforce, because your kids spend all their free time in the family room. So rethink your rule. Maybe it would be better that all toys are to be picked up before anyone goes to bed. That may be a more realistic rule.

Maintaining consistency also applies to your general nature. Most people have mood swings. You know, off days where nothing seems to go right. As adults, we usually let other people's moody days roll off our backs. Kids, however, take your bad moods personally. Living with a schizophrenic can't be fun, so don't make your kids feel like they're living with one.

Following Through by Sticking to Your Word

Following through means doing what you said you were going to do if your child makes a choice to follow an action. It means sticking to your original word, an important offshoot of being consistent.

Before follow-through can happen, you must give your child a choice. Giving children choices keeps you from being a bully and enables them to *make* the choice.

As an example, don't say, "Do that one more time, and you'll regret it." It sounds nice because it gives you an out; you're not bound to do anything linked to that threat. It's better to say, instead, "If you choose to do that one more time, then I'm not allowing A.J. to spend the night tonight."

Then if the child *chooses* to do the dastardly deed one more time, your follow-through is to say, "You chose to do (whatever). Because you made that choice, you don't get to have A.J. spend the night." Then you need to follow through by not allowing A.J. to spend the night.

You gave the child a choice but also put the behavior in his hands. He made a choice, so your follow-through was based on that choice.

That's the gist of following through. But it can be broken down into three major parts:

- ☺ Thinking of the situation before you act and talk (also known as choosing your battles)

- ☺ Doing what you say you're going to do when you tell your child you're going to do something

- ☺ Following up with your child to ensure that she understands why she was disciplined

Choose your battles

This is also known as picking your fights. Children, in their world, make sense. They know why they do things and why it makes sense to do them. They don't always have the verbal skills to explain this to you, but they do make sense.

So before you go barking orders and doling out punishments, try finding out why your child is doing what she is doing. Say you're walking into the living room and your child has all the cushions and pillows off the couch. Before you go ballistic, find out why. She probably has a really good reason. Either a lost toy or the beginning construction stages of a great ship.

When you say you're going to do something, do it

Children need to know that if you say you're going to do something, you do it. That way they can trust what you say — and trust that you're a reliable person. This trust works for good and bad situations.

When you promise to get your children a treat at the store if they clean their rooms, you give them something to work toward. They know you're going to buy them that treat. When, on the other hand, you tell your children that if they start hitting each other, they'll have their toys taken away for the rest of the night, they'll understand you mean that, too.

 Promising to do something (whether it's good or bad) and never doing it makes you look like a flake, even to your kids. Your children need to trust and believe what you say. If they can't trust their parents, they grow up with trust issues the rest of their lives, which spills over into their relationships forever.

 When your kids know that you're not going to stick to your word, your children will be running your life. *That's* the definition of a spoiled child — not one who has too many toys.

☺ ☹ ☹ ☺ ☺ ☹ ☺ ☺ ☹ ☺ ☺ ☹ ☺ ☺ ☹ ☺ ☺

On the flip side, your life will become a heavenly bliss when you
to the point where they understand that when you say you're goi
something, you do it. You don't make threats, and you don't give
warnings.

That said, understand that training your kids to follow your direct
time. It's a learning process for them. It may take several episod
ishing your children for doing something you've told them not to
they get the idea that it just isn't worth it. Then again, your childr
catch on quickly. A lot has to do with that stubbornness gene kid
inherit from their parents.

Ensure that your child understands why you did it

Punishment is not effective when your children don't learn anythi
it, so making sure that your children understand why they were p
for what they did is important.

Never assume that what your children have just done is obviously
them. **Remember:** Kids make sense to themselves, and sometim
rules don't make sense to them. Children often are oblivious to w
they've done anything wrong. That is why you give them a choice
behavior.

Use discipline and punishment as a form of education. You discipl
children so they learn right from wrong. You punish them for the s
reason. (For more about punishment and discipline, see Chapter 1

Chapter 4

Managing Behavior: Your Child's and Your Own!

Behavior management has two parts. The first part is manipulating your children's time and behavior so that they don't have the time — or need — to become involved in situations that make us want to label them as terrible.

In This Chapter

☺ Helping your kids know how to behave by praising behaviors you want to reoccur

☺ Giving your kids plenty of attention by spending quality time together

☺ Scheduling projects and providing activities to keep your kids busy

> ☺ *tip* If you're a sensitive parent who thinks wanting to *manipulate* your children is awful, keep in mind that it just means to guide, direct, or handle.

The second part of behavior management is understanding the behavior. The things your children do make sense to them and, in many cases, are just a natural result of them being children. Your job is finding out what makes sense to your kids. You have to understand the behavior before you can guide, direct, or handle them.

The thought of manipulating your children isn't so bad when you realize that all you're doing is guiding or directing the things they do so they stay out of trouble. The way you guide your kids is to give praise, give plenty of attention, keep idle hands busy, and keep your cool through it all, which is what this chapter is about.

Giving Praise

Kids are often unsure how to act. Here's where you come in. You help your child determine how to behave by praising or rewarding the behaviors that you want to reoccur. You even praise those behaviors that are on the road

to approximating what you want to happen. Gradually, the approximations grow into full-blown actions that hit the mark head-on. This string of inter-actions is how you shape (or mold) behavior.

The reason praise works is that your positive response helps your child feel good about himself. His feeling cheerier about accomplishments increases the likelihood of that behavior occurring again. Educators and psychologists call this sort of interaction *positive reinforcement.*

 Kids love to hear how good they are and that you're proud of them and think they're special. Don't hold out on giving these comments to your kids, because you need to be their best cheerleader. And remember that praise also means giving hugs, kisses, and pats on the back and head when your children do something good.

Focusing on the positive gives you two bonuses:

❋ You put conscious effort into noticing how well your offspring functions.

❋ You pat yourself on the back at his successes, gaining more confidence as a parent who's raising a smart kid.

 Make sure that you expend more time and emotion on appropriate behavior. I've seen kids who continue to be fussy eaters because picking at foods sends Mom or Dad into a tizzy, and the kids love the attention. But if Mom or Dad spent more time and effort noticing how great it is that little sister tries new foods, perhaps big brother would get the idea to join in.

 To be effective, you must offer praise that's not only honest but also specific. Never bluff praise. Kids have radar that detects when you don't mean what you say. As for the specific part, decide which you would rather hear: "That's nice" or "I like the way you wrote the opening paragraph. It's a grabber." The more specific you can be, the better your child knows what you like and want repeated.

Giving Plenty of Attention

Kids love attention, and they find ways to attract it any way they can. When they can't get your attention by doing good things, they do whatever it takes to get your attention. So if the only time you acknowledge that your kids are around is when they do things you've been known to react to, they'll continue doing those deeds. For example, children often walk toward a door, all the time watching their parents to see whether they'll chase after them. To a child, negative attention is better than no attention.

Spending time with your kids is the best way to give them your attention. Regardless of whether you stay at home or work outside the home, you *still* can give quality time to your kids. And quality time doesn't mean the entire family sitting for four hours watching TV. It means turning the TV off (oh lordy, anything but *that!*) and playing games together, reading books, going for walks, raking the yard — anything! (Check out the following section, "Keeping Idle Hands Busy," for more ideas of things you can do.)

Giving kids your attention also means listening to them when they talk. I don't mean halfway listening and saying "uh-huh" at the appropriate spots. I mean sitting down, looking children in the eye, and listening — responding to what they say and asking questions. Be interested. Doing so shows that you're paying attention, even when you say things like "So you say you painted the cat blue? Tell me more about that." Then allow them to answer.

 You don't have to continually buy your kids gifts as a means of letting them know you love them. Time is what they want most from you. You can't buy it anywhere.

Keeping Idle Hands Busy

Kids will look for something to do if you don't provide some sort of entertainment. Okay, so that doesn't mean you have to put on the Las Vegas showgirl feathers — although your kids probably *would* enjoy that. It also doesn't mean that you have to fall off the scale on the other end, never allowing them time to be quiet and creative with their own play. However, when you don't keep kids busy most of the time, they may choose to color on the wall, string toilet paper all over the bathroom, or pull all the towels out of the cabinet.

The key to keeping children busy is scheduling. Schedules are important to kids physically and psychologically. They get up, eat breakfast, eat lunch, and eat dinner. Some go to preschool or daycare, and those who are old enough go to school. But what do they do the rest of the time? You need to fill up some of the empty spots in their schedules with activities. Schools manage so many children that way. Their schedules are filled with organized time and then free time. But their days are filled with activities.

 If your children are kept busy, they can't get into trouble, but keeping busy doesn't mean that you have to enroll your children in every conceivable activity. It simply means keeping them active enough so that they have neither the time nor the need to look for other activities to prevent boredom from setting in.

Projects that connect your kids with the family

The house is clean, and the schoolwork is done. What can you do with your kids now? How about a special project? *Projects* can be either fun, family rituals, or chores that help keep the house clean and instill responsibility.

Here are some ideas:

- **After breakfast, go for a walk around the block.**

- **Every day after lunch, provide an hour of free time before naptime.**

- **Every birthday or holiday, have the kids make personalized cards (this can be for all family and friends).**

- **One hour before bedtime, have everyone pick up toys, books, shoes, and so on.**

- **Hold a mini tea party with crackers and milk before beginning bedtime routines.**

- **Give the kids chores, like putting the silverware away, putting their own laundry in their drawers, and wiping cupboards.** See Table 4-1 for a chore chart you can photocopy, fill in, and use weekly. Chores are great learning tools. Kids discover all kinds of things from sorting laundry (colors and shapes), fixing lunches (cooking, the nutritional value of foods), cleaning the house (health and safety, camaraderie, and motor-skill practice), and planting gardens (environment, insects, plant growth). **Remember:** Your kids don't always have to be learning for time to be valuable. Read books in the same room or have tickle fights. Being close and accomplishing something together goes a long way toward building family togetherness.

- **Go on family outings, which builds bonds and provides time to practice skills learned at home, such as good manners, taking turns, and respect for others.** See Table 4-2 for outing ideas and a checklist you can use.

- **Schedule a family night the same night each week or month.** Plan on spending the time together in some fun activity, such as playing games, taking walks, baking cookies, or going to movies. Or institute backward night, where you wear clothes backward and talk backward, or silly suppers, in which you eat outrageous combinations of food.

- **Volunteer together.** Check out food banks, seniors' homes, homeless shelters, local political offices, or worthwhile organizations that can use help.

- **Have reading time each night.** Someone can read a story aloud, family members can take turns reading aloud, or you can each read what you want.

☺ ☻ ☹ ☺ ☻ ☹ ☺ ☻ ☹ ☺ ☻ ☹ ☺ ☻ ☹ ☺ ☺ ☻ ☹ ☺

Table 4-1 Chore Chart and Check-Off List

Child and His/Her Chores for the Week	Mon	Tues	Wed	Thurs	Fri	Sat	Sun
Child (name)_____							
Child (name)_____							

Table 4-2 Family Outings You Can Try

Outing	Tried It	Do Again!	Comments
Museum	☐	☐	
Store	☐	☐	
Library	☐	☐	
Forest preserve	☐	☐	
Beach	☐	☐	
Apple orchard	☐	☐	
Pumpkin patch	☐	☐	
Bicycle ride	☐	☐	
Other:_____	☐	☐	
Other:_____	☐	☐	
Other:_____	☐	☐	
Other:_____	☐	☐	

Play that moves toddler/preschooler muscles and builds confidence

Toddlers and preschoolers are busy people. The more they do, the greater their confidence that they can climb any mountain. You want to encourage these positive play experiences; they become the seeds of courage that bolster your child's confidence. Here are a couple ways to move your child's muscles and build confidence in the process:

- **Make lots of trips to the playground.** Allow your child to climb, run, spin around, and swing. Try not to be overprotective. Unless your child has particular motor or behavior problems, he usually won't try something he can't handle. But stay close when he climbs higher than usual. Your nearness lends support. You're also nearby just in case you hear an emergency call for help.

- **Buy or make some equipment that exercises large toddler muscles.** Here are some examples: sandbox (big enough for friends), plastic tunnel (it can go inside or outside), dome climber (bonus: your child can throw a sheet over the top and pretend the hollow inside of the dome is a fort, teepee, and such), water play items (large container or wading pool, garden hose, sprinkler, and so on), and a tricycle, tike bike, or other wheeled mode of transportation.

Toys that spark toddler/preschooler imaginations

Two- to five-year-olds love their fantasy play. Through fantasy, your child alters the real world. Fantasy play provides a safe way to experience pretend scary situations and work them out. Play offers a chance to change the frightening into the joyful. Kids test more worldly waters through fantasy without having to get completely submerged.

To encourage your child's imagination, find the following:

- Toys that can be used for more than one thing, like bean bags, a box of wheels and spools to sort and build, clothespins and sticks for craft projects, empty boxes and cans for play and storing, large beads for stringing, large blocks for climbing and building, manipulative toys such as LEGOs, Play-Doh — the list is virtually endless.

- Toys that aren't so delicate that you're constantly hovering over your child, telling him how to use them or showing your displeasure when they are thrown, dropped, or otherwise abused.

You don't need to buy expensive toys for your child to re-create the world. At this stage, your child is old enough to change everyday items into play props. For example:

☺ ☺ ☹ ☺ ☺ ☹ ☺ ☺ ☹ ☺ ☺ ☹ ☺ ☺ ☹ ☺ ☺ ☹ ☹ ☺

- A washing-machine box made into a fort in the living room

- Your old clothes worn as dress-up costumes

- A towel transformed into a superhero cape

- Boats made from blocks that help imaginary friends sail to magical islands in search of fantastic treasures

These props allow your toddler to

- **Stay entertained for hours:** He'll play alongside others throughout his second year, not really interested in much sharing at that point. By about age 3, however, your little introvert may blossom into a social butterfly, playing with others the same age and pushing, shoving, and squabbling with the best of them.

- **Express emotions:** Your child acts out everything from personal feelings to what transpires between members of the household. So watch out! You're in for eye-opening views into how family interactions, jobs, and roles are perceived by your child.

Resources for planning fun and well-rounded activities

Besides local religious (YMCA, YWCA, JCC) and public community centers, these groups promote programs your child may like:

- **Association of Children's Museums** (1300 L Street, NW, Suite 975, Washington, DC 20005, phone: 202-898-1080, Internet: www. childrensmuseums.org): Although this group serves the museum community first, its Web site lets you search for children's museums near you and connect with their sites to find out what's happening at those museums.

- **Boys and Girls Clubs of America** (1230 West Peachtree Street, NW, Atlanta, GA 30309, phone: 404-487-5700, Internet: www.bgca. org): These clubs are everywhere, and they provide interesting programs to stimulate the interests of kids.

- **Girls Scouts of the USA** (420 Fifth Avenue, New York, NY, 10018, phone: 800-478-7248, Internet: www.girlscouts.org): Girl Scouts maintain more than 230,000 troops in the United States for girls 5 to 17 years old. Their job is to develop potential through field trips, sports, community service, cultural exchanges, and environmental programs.

- **Boys Scouts of America** (P.O. Box 152079, Irving, TX 75015-2079, Internet: www.scouting.org): This organization groups boys into Cub Scouts (ages 7 to 10) and Boy Scouts (ages 11 to 17). Through regular meetings and outdoor activities, Boy Scouts of America provides fun activities, teaches leadership and community service skills, and inspires high morals and personal growth. Check your phone book for a local council office.

* **Camp Fire USA** (4601 Madison Avenue, Kansas City, MO 64112-1278, phone: 816-756-0258, Internet: www.campfire.org). This national youth-development organization serves kids from birth to age 21 with childcare, after-school programs, and camping and environmental programs designed to build self-reliance and foster intercultural relationships.

Keeping Your Cool with the Kids

How are you going to act when you find that your 3-year-old daughter has just emptied a whole bottle of perfume all over herself and has smeared lipstick completely over her face, your walls, and maybe even the cat who happened to get in her way, all for the sake of being pretty like Mommy? Do you

* Lose all the color from your face, whisk your daughter up, and throw her into the bathtub?

* Say "Don't you look pretty. How about we get you all cleaned up? The next time you play dressup, why don't you ask me, and I'll help you?"

* Look at your daughter, heave a sigh, and then turn around and leave?

If you're scratching your head, the answer is the second choice. Parents who respond the second way are dealing with their child in a calm, relaxed way — at the same time getting the point across that the child shouldn't do what she's done again without supervision.

Not having patience may stem somewhat from your own upbringing. Your parents may not have had much patience, so you weren't able to learn from them. Although your inner "coolness" is there just waiting to come out, maybe it can't because of things you're overlooking:

* **Your attitude:** Having patience begins with your attitude. If you're a perfectionist, now is the time to get over it. Not until your kids are grown and out of the house will everything be sane, clean, and in order (at least not all at the same time). When you can adopt the attitude that it's all going to be okay — and you can deal with it for about 18 years — you're ahead of the game. **Remember:** Don't take things too seriously. Allow kids to be kids and do the goofy things that they're supposed to do — make messes, drop and break things, spill, topple, destroy, mutilate. If you accept the fact that these things will happen, you won't lose your patience when they do.

* **The reasoning behind the action:** Your kids make sense. It's up to you to find out what *their* sense is. Doing so is one way of finding patience. When you look at your kids in a more curious manner — such as, "Wow, that was rather creative. Tell me more about why you colored on the walls" — then their actions can be put into a better perspective.

☺ ☺ ☹ ☺ ☺ ☹ ☺ ☺ ☹ ☺ ☺ ☹ ☺ ☺ ☹ ☺ ☺ ☹ ☺

❋ **How you feel:** You lose your patience because you're too tired and too stressed to find the real meaning behind your child's actions. Many parents also have a building resentment when they feel they're being overworked without any help, and they don't have enough time for themselves. If you find yourself in this boat, work to change your life so these situations don't happen. Go to bed earlier and turn off the television. Schedule chores so everyone helps. Schedule alone time so you can reconnect with yourself.

❋ **Unrealistic expectations:** You may lose patience because the expectations you have for your kids are unrealistic. You can't expect your 5-year-old to sit quietly through all your favorite parts of *Gone with the Wind,* nor can you expect your 1-year-old to remember to stay out of the toilet paper even though you've told him at least 50 times. Don't expect your kids to listen to you the same way in all situations and don't expect miracles from them.

❋ **Not taking the responsibility yourself:** Take responsibility when your toddler gets into the litter box because you didn't shut the door. Your toddler doesn't know that litter box sand and beach sand are different. You have to be responsible enough to create an environment where your kids aren't in constant trouble because you don't put things away.

❋ **Feeling rushed or hurried:** Patience runs short when time runs short. Being late can drive some people insane, and they take everyone to the asylum with them. If you're that way, you can solve the problem by giving yourself plenty of time to do things and get to places. Do as much advance planning as possible.

Managing parent ego: Yes, yours!

Stay alert to what's important about raising your child: nurturing a confident, independent person who likes herself. Remember that parenting is *not* about

● **Growing an extension of yourself:** Check your ego at the door if you prefer a child who dances but your child loves racing cars instead. This is her life.

● **Creating a status symbol:** Your child has not been put on this Earth to glorify you. If you have a high achiever, remember the little person inside. She doesn't exist so you can brag about grades, test scores, or the number of batters she strikes out.

● **Smothering your child in the name of love:** Your child should not be the total focus of your existence. Yes, your child takes considerable time and energy, not to mention loving. But she needs some space in order to ever be able to separate from you.

That said, do remember that smart parenting involves being proud of your child. Give liberal amounts of love and respect!

Part 2

Dealing with the "Easy" Stuff: Physical Development

The chapters in this part are all about the physical development of your child — growth and milestones, diet and exercise, sleep and bedtime issues, and that fun time for all: potty training.

This part is honest about the struggles you'll encounter, and it empowers you with the knowledge that the rough times do pass. Kids eventually do sleep through the night, for example, and graduate from potty-training school.

Chapter 5

But That Shirt Fit Yesterday!: Your Child's Growth

Children go through definite stages of development. Babies roll over, sit, and usually crawl before walking. School-age youngsters learn counting to 100 and addition before being expected to multiply and handle percentages. Milestones occur generally around the same time for most kids, although all kids vary, which is totally normal.

Recognizing that children go through stages of development makes parenting easier because the information creates more realistic expectations. Realizing that everyone goes through stages helps you guide your kid wisely because you have an idea what childhood is about.

Moving from one developmental stage to another isn't life altering. A little frustration at one step or another doesn't scar your child for life or produce a mentally unbalanced adult. Most stages are part of the natural evolution of growth and maturation. You've passed through numerous phases in your life and probably will go through still more. Your kids will move along just fine, too.

Understand, too, that not every child goes through every stage. Some kids skip crawling and leap right to standing and walking. Moreover, your child may go through the same stage later or earlier than her best buddy. Does this mean your child has a problem? Probably not. This merely means your child is following her own timeframe for developing, and that's okay.

The same advice applies to children's weight and height. Growth varies tremendously from child to child and is influenced by many factors, including nutrition, fitness, and family genes. This chapter presents very general growth ranges at various ages, and your child may or may not fall into them. Your child's doctor will keep tabs on your child's personal growth, checking height and weight at each visit. If your doctor has concerns, he will let you know and discuss possible causes and solutions. Likewise, if you have concerns, bring them up to your doctor.

Toddler Milestones

This section covers some general growth and development milestones for children from about 10 to 24 months of age.

General development

At 10 months of age, your baby begins turning into a toddler. He can stand if he holds on to someone or something, and he can pull himself to a standing position.

Eleven months marks the coming of the gentle sounds of *mama, dada,* and *no.* (In one more month, these words will become more specific and clear.) Clapping hands and waving good-bye are typical of an 11-month-old. Expect frequent tumbles and falls as he practices his balancing skills.

tip

Babyproof your house *now,* if you haven't yet done so. Investing in soft, cushioned, corner guards for sharp table edges is a good idea. Don't forget that little fingers are able to reach into drawers and cabinets, so make sure that you have locks on them, too. Keep hot or otherwise dangerous objects safely out of reach, away from table and counter edges. Now is also a good time to turn your water heater temperature down to 120° F to help prevent burn injuries. Little ones can grab the hot water knob and severely hurt themselves. (Check out Chapter 16 for more safety tips.)

One year is a true milestone for many parents. Your young lad is probably very active. He's probably dancing, walking around holding furniture, pushing and pulling and dumping toys, pulling off hats and socks, and even identifying himself in the mirror. And your doctor is going to want to know answers to the following developmental questions:

- Does he pull himself up to stand?
- Can he walk around holding on to furniture?
- Does he wave "bye-bye"?

* Can he say any words? What are they?

* Can he imitate sounds (like animal sounds)?

Tradition is that you don't give your child his first haircut until his first birthday, which is a major photo op for many parents. That first haircut marks the transition from baby to little boy or little girl.

Fifteen months often marks a time when you can first *see* the little boy or girl in the baby you've known. Here are the developmental questions you'll be asked at your toddler's 15-month checkup:

* Can he perform hand-eye-coordinated tasks like building a tower of blocks?

* Can he walk without help?

* Does he use a spoon?

* Does he understand a one-step command, such as "Bring me the box"?

* Have his language skills increased to several words?

From 15 to 18 months, your toddler begins naming several common objects, or at least says close approximations. He begins to repeat what you say and points to let you know what he wants. In addition, he walks alone, pulls toys, shows an interest in turning book pages, fits two-piece puzzles, and tries to throw.

By the time your toddler is 18 to 24 months old, he's come a long way. He says up to 300 words. He makes two-word sentences and puts emotion into talking. He scribbles with crayons, actually turns those book pages, runs without falling, fits five-piece puzzles, and masters those stairs.

Toddlers learn to use the potty between 2 and 4 years of age. If that span seems kind of old to you, keep in mind that not until between the ages of 18 and 24 months do toddlers begin recognizing what it feels like when they have to go to the bathroom. Before then, these bodily functions just sort of magically happen.

General growth

When it comes to your child's physical growth, keep in mind that it's influenced by many things, including diet, exercise, gender, and genetic background. In other words, your child is unique and may not fit standardized averages. At each of your child's doctor visits, your doctor will meticulously plot your child's weight and height on a growth chart and show you where your child's height and weight fall within the chart's specific ranges. If you have any concerns about your child's physical growth, talk with your doctor.

That said, here are some very general growth guidelines for the milestone ages of 12 months and 24 months:

❀ By the time babies are 12 months old, they've typically tripled their birth weights. Your child may weigh about 19 to 27 pounds, and he may measure about 28 to 31 inches in length.

❀ By the time your child is 24 months old, he may weigh about 21 to 35 pounds and may measure about 32 to 38 inches in length.

Preschooler Milestones

This section covers some general growth and development milestones for children ages 3 to 5.

General development

At 3 years old, your preschooler's language skills include playing with words, combining four- to five-word sentences, and having approximately a 900-word vocabulary. As for her senses and motor skills, she pedals her tricycle, puts on her shoes, feeds herself without many spills, paints, and pastes. In addition, her social and mental activities including showing independence, cooperating, beginning to make decisions, and playing cooperatively. She may also develop an imaginary playmate.

At 4 years old, your preschooler's language skills include questioning *everything*, giving orders, using a 1,500-word vocabulary, and loving potty talk and word games. In addition, she may stutter. Her senses and motor skills include tracing, sewing cards, helping with chores, and cutting with scissors. And on the social and mental fronts, she becomes more social, fixates on routines, demands and brags, rhymes, loves to tell stories, and loves being silly.

By the time she's 5 years old, her language skills have come a long way. She defines things realistically and uses a 2,200-word vocabulary! Her senses and motor skills have progressed tremendously, too. She jumps rope, uses the toilet unassisted, dresses herself, skates, and colors within the lines. Her social and mental activities include moving around the neighborhood by herself, matching and sorting, knowing what's missing, and completing activities.

General growth

When it comes to your child's physical growth, keep in mind that it's influenced by many things, including diet, exercise, gender, and genetic background. In other words, your child is unique and may not fit standardized averages. At each of your child's doctor visits, your doctor will meticulously plot your child's weight and height on a growth chart and show you where your child's height and weight fall within the chart's specific ranges. If you have any concerns about your child's physical growth, talk with your doctor.

That said, here are some very general growth guidelines for ages 3 to 5:

❋ By the time your child is 3 years old, she may weigh about 28 to 38 pounds and may measure about 35 to 40 inches tall.

❋ By the time your child is 4 years old, she may weigh about 32 to 45 pounds and may measure about 37 to 45 inches tall.

❋ By the time your child is 5 years old, she may weigh about 36 to 55 pounds and may measure about 40 to 46 inches tall.

School-Age Milestones

This section covers some general growth and development milestones for children ages 5 to 12.

School readiness skills

A range of skills and behaviors encompass school readiness. These skills serve as guidelines to help you prepare your child for big-kid school. This section isn't meant to cause hysteria if your child doesn't perform this or that task. With time, your child will accomplish most of the items by practicing them naturally during school and during your regular family activities.

Encourage your child to acquire at least rudimentary knowledge of these 12 important social skills:

❋ Separating from you and home without getting bent out of shape

❋ Recognizing that different people and places have different rules

❋ Following rules at home and at other places

❋ Listening quietly and paying attention

❋ Playing and working as part of a group

❋ Understanding that others have feelings and rights

* Taking turns
* Respecting what belongs to someone else
* Sharing
* Controlling impulses, such as temper outbursts or hitting
* Delaying gratification, such as waiting for snack or outdoor time
* Liking or acting curious about new experiences and having the confidence to explore them

Readiness involves every aspect of development. In the olden days, the skills in Table 5-1 were lumped under the single heading called *reading readiness*. That's because reading is the soul of education. Today, you find teachers invoking that term or talking about general readiness for school.

Table 5-1 The Scoop on Readiness Skills

Reading	Fine and Large Motor	Math/Science
Knows what letters are	Draws, scribbles with crayons	Counts from 1 to 10
Names alphabet	Buttons, snaps, zips	Counts some objects
Recognizes name	Assembles easy puzzles	Matches by color, shape, size
Identifies colors	Cuts with rounded scissors	Names basic shapes
Recounts stories	Laces, strings beads	Sorts by color, shape, size
Identifies rhymes	Copies simple shapes, letters	Knows money buys things
Asks questions	Pedals a tricycle	Knows position concepts (up, down, under, over)
Makes up stories	Hops on one foot briefly	Knows quality concepts (hot, cold, hard, soft)
Follows three-step directions	Alternates feet on stairs	Grasps idea of time (night, day, today, tomorrow, now, later)
Names common animals	Pastes, models clay	Appreciates nature
Enjoys stories and books	Throws, catches, kicks a ball	Knows full and empty

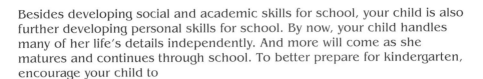

Besides developing social and academic skills for school, your child is also further developing personal skills for school. By now, your child handles many of her life's details independently. And more will come as she matures and continues through school. To better prepare for kindergarten, encourage your child to

- **Manage basic eating routines by herself.** Bring on the chores here. Besides eating with a spoon and fork, give your child practice in pouring water into a glass, spreading peanut butter and jelly, carrying food and drinks without spilling, and cleaning up after herself. Neither you nor a teacher expect perfection. But the opportunity to complete a task and take care of herself builds confidence and makes life much easier for you and the busy kindergarten teacher.

- **Master toileting and washing.** Give your child practice going to the bathroom in public places so that the school bathroom won't intimidate her. Make sure your child knows the entire routine: taking down and pulling up clothes, wiping afterward, flushing the toilet, and washing afterward. Add some urinal practice for your son.

- **Conquer the ins and outs of dressing.** Remember to practice zippers, buttons, and testy boots. The ability to tie shoelaces is great, but that skill may be difficult for little fingers now. If being unable to tie shoelaces bothers your child, find shoes with Velcro fasteners. And one-zip, one-piece clothing often simplifies the dressing process. If you live in snowy territory, teach your youngster to place a plastic bag over each shoe before inserting it into a snug boot. The shoe slides in without all those pulls and tugs that drive kids and teachers crazy.

- **Know the basics about herself and her family.** Practice with your child to ensure she knows her full name, address, telephone number, age, gender, and body parts. Make sure she knows the names of family members and the fact that the dog isn't really a sibling, no matter how close they are. Some teachers lack a sense of humor.

Skills learned through friends

During early elementary years, your child chooses friends based on what they can do together. By ages 8 to 10, relationships deepen to include lengthier conversations, loyalty, and helpfulness. These closer bonds are critical for maturation and a sense of identity that bolsters book learning.

From friends, your child learns skills for achieving success in today's school and work world:

❀ How to negotiate and cooperate

❀ How to navigate group norms and rules

❀ How to be responsible to more than oneself; in other words, how to be sociable and caring

❀ How to feel part of another group besides family

General growth

When it comes to your child's physical growth, keep in mind that it's influenced by many things, including diet, exercise, gender, and genetic background. In other words, your child is unique and may not fit standardized averages. At each of your child's doctor visits, your doctor will meticulously plot your child's weight and height on a growth chart and show you where your child's height and weight fall within the chart's specific ranges. If you have any concerns about your child's physical growth, talk with your doctor.

That said, here are some very general growth guidelines for children ages 6 to 8:

❀ By the time your child is 6 years old, she may weigh about 38 to 65 pounds and may measure about 42 to 48 inches tall.

❀ By the time your child is 7 years old, she may weigh about 43 to 70 pounds and may measure about 44 to 51 inches tall.

❀ By the time your child is 8 years old, she may weigh about 50 to 78 pounds and may measure about 45 to 55 inches tall.

From age 9 until puberty hits, you can expect your child to keep gaining weight and height steadily — around 5 to 10 pounds a year and 2 to 3 (give or take) inches. Keep in mind, though, that in these later school-age years, *major* growth spurts can happen in any given year.

Puberty

By the end of eighth grade, you can expect to see lots of physical changes in your child. Your child gains an average of 2½ inches and 7 pounds each year. That comes with doubled muscle mass and more strength than you're used to. You can't just pick up and deposit your child somewhere, should he act evil.

☺ ☺ ☹ ☺ ☺ ☹ ☺ ☺ ☹ ☺ ☺ ☹ ☺ ☺ ☺ ☹ ☺

In addition, your child notices body changes in other young people that fall into two categories: his and hers. Playgroups separate by gender, which is good because hormones begin to pulsate in junior high.

Your child is now capable of reading, writing, paying attention, and abstract thinking, too, so prepare for great debates when you won't cough up money or disagree about study habits.

In short, your child is crossing over the maturational bridge between childhood and adulthood. This stage is called *adolescence,* or the teenage years, and some general physical changes occur during this time in your child's life:

* *Puberty,* the body's route to being able to reproduce, extends over three to four years. Although age of onset varies, girls usually undergo puberty earlier than boys.

* Body clock shifts to a later setting.

* Bones and muscles mature to almost adult size. But coordination and strength decreases for a time because bones are growing faster than muscles.

* Sex-linked hormones cause related body changes, even dreaded acne.

* Brain growth continues through adolescence, which is why interference from mind-altering substances (drugs) can short-circuit wiring so easily.

Puberty in girls

Here's what you can expect with girls during puberty:

* Puberty begins between ages 8 and 13.

* Menstrual cycle starts during puberty. This is a terrifying sign that your daughter is ready to conceive and carry a baby (though she may be physically, she's really not emotionally or otherwise). The hormone estrogen causes periods when ovaries release eggs into fallopian tubes. Thus begins a monthly cycle that runs 400 times over the course of her lifetime.

* Skeleton grows in a specific order, unlike male bodies. First, hands and feet expand. Then forearms and shins. Finally, upper arms and thighs. After menstruation begins, leg bones usually stop growing, but hipbones widen and the spine continues to elongate until the body achieves adult height.

❀ Womanly curves appear. Breasts develop.

❀ Hair sprouts under arms and in the pubic area.

Puberty in boys

Here's what you can expect with boys during puberty:

❀ Puberty begins between ages 10 and 14.

❀ Testicles produce greater amounts of the hormone testosterone. The sex-related hormone changes the size and texture of the testicles. By age 15, this pair of glands has increased 400 percent and can produce 1,000 sperm per second.

❀ Shoulders widen. Jaw and nose bones grow faster than the rest of the face, winding up with the chiseled jaw of a man.

❀ Voice deepens.

❀ Hair develops under arms, on the face, neck, and chest, and in the pubic area.

Your Own Child's Milestones

Want a handy place to track the general growth and development milestones of your own child? Use Table 5-2 (and feel free to make copies if you have more than one child). Write your child's name in the space provided at the top and then record your child's height and weight at each milestone age. Then, whenever you want, jot down various physical milestones he or she has accomplished, along with the date.

Table 5-2 Physical Growth and Milestones of _____				
Age	Height	Weight	Date	Milestones
10 months	_____	_____	_____	_____ _____ _____ _____ _____ _____ _____ _____ _____

Chapter 5: Your Child's Growth

Age	Height	Weight	Date	Milestones
11 months	_____	_____	_____	
1 year	_____	_____	_____	
2 years	_____	_____	_____	
3 years	_____	_____	_____	
4 years	_____	_____	_____	

Age	Height	Weight	Date	Milestones
5 years	_____	_____	_____	_____
6 years	_____	_____	_____	_____
7 years	_____	_____	_____	_____
8 years	_____	_____	_____	_____

Chapter **6**

Nurturing a Healthy Body and Mind

Food and fitness are essentials for a healthy body and mind. Food furnishes the fuel that keeps kids healthy. By providing a variety of good foods, your child receives enough essential vitamins and minerals to be able to think, remember, and reason (and have enough energy to stay awake in class). Likewise, fitness promotes physical and mental health, and the bonus is that physical activity improves self-confidence and self-discipline.

This chapter offers suggestions for making healthy eating, fitness, and physical activity part of your kids' everyday lives.

Establishing Healthy Eating Habits

Your children will go through several food stages during their lives. Besides mood swings during puberty, nothing will be more disturbing than the changes that kids go through with their eating habits.

This fluctuation is disturbing to parents because eating changes can be rather dramatic. One day you think your child has a hollow leg and can't seem to get enough to eat. The next day, she may not be interested in food at all.

Trust your children. They know how much they need to eat. When they don't clean their plates, trust that they've had enough to eat. If they keep asking for more food, by all means shovel it in. As long as you're giving them healthy foods, they should be allowed to eat as much as they want. They'll stop when they're finished.

 Your children are unique. They grow at a different rate than other children. Their eating habits also probably won't match any food chart you've read. Changes in eating habits not only include the amount your children want to eat but also the times at which they eat. Don't be surprised when they aren't hungry at dinnertime, but 30 minutes later, they complain that they're starving.

Keeping all these things in mind, your role is to provide nutritious foods and instill healthy eating habits. That's what this section is all about.

Choosing healthy brain foods

Prepare a variety of foods for your family so that all the healthy stuff is available. Be sure to give your child a balanced diet that includes grains, fruits and vegetables, dairy products, and some form of meat or meat substitute. Check out the food pyramid in Figure 6-1 as a starting point for getting your kid on the right diet track.

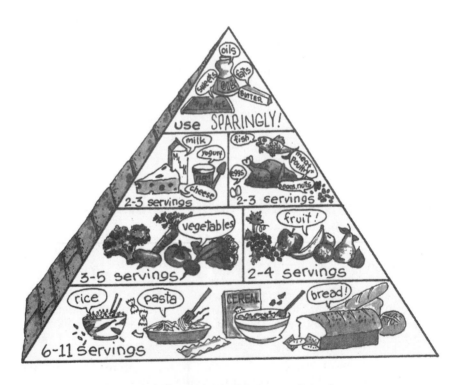

Figure 6-1: The food pyramid is a great help when you're deciding what to feed your kids.

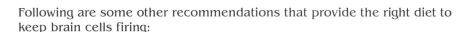
Following are some other recommendations that provide the right diet to keep brain cells firing:

❋ **Offer a nutritious breakfast.** Even if your child hates to have breakfast, start her day off energized instead of droopy with at least small amounts of protein and grains.

❋ **Supply healthy lunches with nutritious desserts and snacks.** Check out the nutritional guidelines article at www.parentsplace.com for healthy lunchbox ideas.

❋ **Remember to include iron-rich foods.** Studies show that kids with iron deficiencies score lower than their iron-rich classmates on math tests and are more irritable, tired, and unable to concentrate. Good sources of iron are red meat, poultry, beans, and whole grains.

❋ **Include plenty of water in everyone's diet.** Usual recommendations of six to eight 8-ounce glasses a day keep the body, and especially the brain, well lubricated.

❋ **Never buy soda pop.** Soda is mainly sugar water with a bunch of chemicals that rot your teeth and provide loads of empty calories. And then there's the inevitable crashing of your kid's brain after the sugar rush. This happens when sugar levels in the blood that feeds the brain become elevated from the surge of sugar and then drop suddenly, leaving the brain with fewer nutrients to function. If soda isn't around the house, your child won't get used to drinking it.

❋ **Limit sweets.** Sugary and junk foods, like fatty chips, provide empty calories that cause brain rushes and crashes and add too many calories that contribute to weight gain. Sweets once in a while aren't the worst thing in the world. But having large amounts of sweets and junk food around regularly is more temptation than anyone needs.

❋ **Limit trips to fast-food restaurants.** Time is precious, but fast-food restaurants process the few vitamins and minerals the food originally has out of them. And they douse your food with too many unhealthy fats, salt, and sugars.

❋ **Read labels to omit unhealthy types of fats from the family diet.** Certain kinds of fat cause health problems, such as high cholesterol and arterial disease. If you have a choice, choose non-animal-based monounsaturates and polyunsaturates over animal-based saturated fats. Also avoid the trans fats that are in hydrogenated vegetable oils. The way the oil is processed changes its character, turning it into a cholesterol-builder. One way to tell what's saturated fat and trans fat is to discover whether it hardens at room temperature, like butter (saturated fat) and many types of peanut butter (hydrogenated oils). Also read labels, which list many types of fats and show hydrogenated oils in the ingredients list.

❀ **Turn off the tube.** Television projects disproportionate amounts of time per show of hard-sell commercials for fast foods and sugar-laden foods. If your child watches TV, take some time to go over what commercials aim to do and why so that she becomes a savvy consumer early on. (Heavy-duty commercialism invades most kids' magazines, too, so stay vigilant.)

 Your job is to raise a child who knows how to make wise food choices that keep her body in tip-top shape. These healthy eating habits your child masters at a young age contribute to a lifetime of success.

In addition, know that your children will learn good eating habits not only from what you feed them but also by what they observe. You need to have good eating habits, and so do older siblings. If baby sees her older sister eating chocolate Pop Tarts for breakfast, she'll want to eat them, too.

Avoiding the picky-eater syndrome

Your kids are going to turn their noses up at some of the foods that you offer. Depending on your children (because they're all different), they may refuse everything you put in front of them or they may rarely sneer at food. Toddlers are especially good at being picky eaters.

Here are some things you can do to avoid raising a picky eater:

❀ **Introduce a wide variety of foods.** Giving your kids a wide variety of foods at a young age offers them an opportunity to experiment with food and find more things that they like. It also makes them more open to trying different foods. Take more time at the grocery store and actually look at all the different types of food instead of always reaching for your regular items. And take the time to experiment with new flavors or textures.

❀ **Don't give up on a food after one try.** If your kids snub carrots, don't give them a candy bar as a replacement. Just give them another vegetable. Offer them carrots again in a week or so. If they still don't like carrots, offer them again in another six months. The kids may have a different attitude about them at that time. Sometimes you have to offer foods more than ten times before a child will give the food a try.

❀ **Leave warfare out of mealtime.** Dinner shouldn't be a battle zone pitting you and your children against each other. Keep in mind that as people grow up, their taste buds develop and food has more of a flavor than when they were younger. Much of the food little kids are offered doesn't really have much of a flavor. That's why kids love sweets so much. The flavor is strong, and they can taste it.

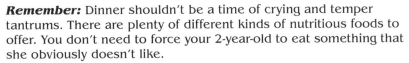

Remember: Dinner shouldn't be a time of crying and temper tantrums. There are plenty of different kinds of nutritious foods to offer. You don't need to force your 2-year-old to eat something that she obviously doesn't like.

✿ **Don't overwhelm your child with too much food on her plate.** A good rule of thumb is to give your child 1 tablespoon per year of age.

If you have a child who tends to reject food, try making the food look fun. Cut sandwiches into shapes, arrange corn in the shape of a heart, or serve it in a plastic toy (washing the toy first, of course). Do whatever you can think of to make meals more fun.

Dieting

As your children grow, they may seem chunkier at times, and then they'll slim down. Such fluctuations are normal. If you're concerned, however, that your children are too thin or too heavy, talk to your doctor.

Unless specified by your doctor, though, the only "diet" your children need to be on is a normal, healthy, eating-the-right-kind-of-foods diet. Don't count the calories or fat grams for children. Just keep them away from sugars, fast foods (grease), junk food (crackers, chips, candy), and too much processed meats (like hot dogs and bologna), and they'll be fine. Doing that may sound impossible, but if you make the effort, you'll at least reduce the intake of these foods considerably.

Don't automatically put your child on a low-fat or no-fat diet. Children under 2 years old do not need dietary fat restrictions. They need fat and cholesterol for the brain and nervous system development. If your children are older than 2 years of age, you can start cutting some of the fat out of their diets. They can be on the same diet as an adult, as recommended by the American Heart Association (no more than 20 percent of calories from fat). Follow the food pyramid (refer to Figure 6-1). But you can also buy low-fat milk or low-fat yogurt, for example. Get rid of the bad fat, not the good fat. Bad fats are those found in chips. Good fats are those in avocados and olive oil. For lots more choices, take a look at www.americanheart.org.

Many foods that are advertised as low-fat actually are high in sugar, which is of no benefit. Keep your kids on a naturally low-fat diet by giving them plenty of fruits and vegetables. It's the best solution to the diet dilemma.

Snacking

Your children's bodies are unable to consume enough during one meal to last until the next. So let them snack. Work in those fruits and vegetables for snacks. The word *snack* doesn't have to imply junk food.

Plan to feed your children three meals and two or three snacks a day. These snacks are needed to help balance their diets and give them energy. But keep in mind that children after the age of 12 months often decide they don't like three meals a day. Some children take only one meal per day and then are happy with several small meals or snacks during the day. Don't worry. This behavior is normal. Just make sure the small meals or snacks are healthy foods.

If you don't like the idea of cooking for a child who just takes two bites and then runs off, give her small portions on the plate and refrigerate the rest. When she's ready to eat again, give her the rest of the meal.

Dealing with moodiness, crankiness, and hyperactivity

If your child tends to have mood swings or gets cranky easily, it may be caused by her blood sugar going up and down. Diet is the reason for this. Eating foods that are high in carbohydrates and sugar is one of the reasons everyone tends to be moody, tired, and easily upset. Foods that are high in carbohydrates and sugar are presweetened cereals, crackers, cookies, cakes, and ice cream (basically all the good stuff that makes life worth living). Reduce the carbohydrates and raise the amount of proteins that your children take in.

Moodiness, crankiness, or hyperactive behavior can also be caused by food allergies. Allergies to food don't necessarily involve breaking out in little red bumps all over one's body. Allergies can also alter behavior. For example, your docile, sweet child may be fine all morning until lunch. But after he eats a peanut butter and jelly sandwich, you may find yourself peeling the kid off the wall. This kind of behavior can be a reaction to the bread, the peanut butter, or the jelly.

If you suspect that your child is allergic to some sort of food, you can try your own at-home test. Take your child off all processed foods, sugars, and anything with food coloring. Your child will then be on a protein, fruit, and vegetable diet. See how your child does. If she doesn't seem to have any problems, slowly start adding foods, one by one, to the diet, observing how she reacts to each change. If this seems like a long process, you may want to take your child to the doctor and let an expert know your concerns. The doctor can give your child a series of tests to look for any food allergies.

Taking precautions against food poisoning

Federal officials say that 5,000 people die in the United States every year because of food poisoning. Children are among the people most at risk for serious illness from food poisoning, so protect your child by following these precautions:

- ❀ Wash all fruits and vegetables before cooking or serving raw.

- ❀ Don't give your child undercooked poultry, meat, fish, or eggs.

- ❀ Wash your hands, utensils, and kitchen surfaces after handling uncooked poultry and meat.

- ❀ Don't eat rare meat.

- ❀ Promptly refrigerate leftovers.

- ❀ Don't leave foods at room temperature for more than a few hours.

- ❀ Defrost foods in the refrigerator (instead of leaving them on the counter or in the sink to defrost).

- ❀ Keep your refrigerator set to at least 40° F and your freezer to 0° F to keep your food properly refrigerated.

- ❀ Never eat raw eggs.

- ❀ Don't eat or drink anything that smells or looks bad.

- ❀ Don't guess about your safety. If you aren't sure whether food is still good, throw it out!

Making Fitness Part of Your Kids' Lives

Fitness promotes physical *and* mental health, and physical activity improves self-confidence and self-discipline. Those are some great reasons for getting your kids off the couch for exercise. And if those reasons aren't enough, there's more: Without regular activity, your child may face a lifetime of weight problems, illness, and slower motor development.

Creating a fit, healthy environment at home

As the prime family role model and rule maker, show your child that you believe in physical activity and its contribution to living smart by doing the following:

- ❀ **Plan a family physical activity at least once a week.** Try walking through a forest, bicycling, skating, picking strawberries, or challenging another family to a baseball game.

- **Encourage your child to try different individual or team activities.** Help her find something she enjoys enough to stick with it.

- **Participate in regular activity yourself.** Show your kids how exercise can be a lifelong activity. Start your own physical fitness program. If you don't like exercise, try parking a little farther from the store so you have to walk, dancing around the house to your favorite song, or parking your shopping cart in one aisle while you run up and down the aisles to get individual foods. Every little bit helps.

- **Offer physical activity as a reward.** Instead of giving your child a cookie for a job well done, set up a trip to the playground or a bicycle ride together.

- **Assign chores that involve physical activity,** such as raking leaves, mowing the lawn, gardening, and vacuuming the house.

- **Unplug the television, video games, and computer.** If your child must be a viewer, alternate these inactive forms of play with physical activity.

Why fitness builds brighter kids

Research supports the connection between physical activity and mental capabilities. Some long-range studies have been the basis of Title IX, the law that requires schools to give girls the same opportunities and budgets for programs as boys to participate in sports.

Research supports the following facts and figures:

- Aerobic activities, the kind that are vigorous enough to boost your heart rate, increase the amount of oxygen sent to the brain. No, your active child isn't an airhead after exercise, but she does have more neurons firing from the extra oxygen, which helps with thinking and memory.

- Kids who get 240 minutes per week in physical activity earn higher math scores.

- According to the Institute for Athletics and Education and the President's Council on Physical Fitness, active girls earn better grades than their less-active sisters. In fact, physically active girls are three times more likely to graduate from high school than their couch-potato counterparts. These figures relate to boys, too.

- Eighty percent of women leaders in the top 500 U.S. companies have participated in sports, according to the Big Ten Conference.

Sports make kids feel better about themselves. Now that's an easy, low-cost investment in your child's future.

Child-friendly aerobic exercise

Shake those bones and jostle a few brain cells by choosing any of the following (or any other) smart ways to exercise:

* Bicycling
* Cross-country skiing
* Dancing
* Ice skating
* Inline skating
* Jumping rope
* Running in place
* Running outside
* Running up and down stairs
* Sledding
* Swimming
* Tobogganing
* Walking

Getting physical education at school

Visit your child's school and find out what kind of physical fitness your child receives, if any. Your school's program should expose kids to a fun mix of sports, dance, and exercise activities. Numbers differ about the optimum length of time per week, but figure at least 30-minute periods, preferably daily, to allow enough time for kids to drag themselves into the gym and dawdle back to class.

Don't be surprised if physical activity is minimal at best, with school budgets being what they are. If that's the case, you need to decide whether you have the stamina and persistence to try to move school bureaucratic mountains to get programs reinstated. Should you remain undaunted by the task, try some of the following options:

❀ **Talk with the principal about adding physical activities.**
Propose extending in-class physical time or sharing a physical education teacher with another school, if budgets don't allow hiring a full-time PE teacher.

- **Work through your local parent-teacher organization to institute change.** See whether pressure from a vocal and interested group makes a difference. Check whether your PTO or PTA raises funds that could go toward physical education.

- **Contact the district superintendent.** Make a case for the benefits of physical activity for kids. Even though school budgets are tight, perhaps a creative superintendent can come up with alternatives that benefit your child.

- **Keep up with legislation.** Some national politicians keep trying to roll back Title IX, which could give local schools ammunition for cutting girls' teams. (Title IX is the law that requires schools to give girls the same opportunities and budgets for programs as boys to participate in sports.) Lobby your state congressperson to introduce and pass a bill requiring regular physical education in schools.

- **Push for recess every day so that kids can at least run around and play.** Playing games, playing tag, and chasing each other around a playground count as physical activity, too.

- **Suggest after-school athletic programs, which work best with older students.** Sometimes money for extracurricular programs becomes available through sources other than the education budget.

Chapter 7

Getting Good Sleep without Relying on Sheep

This chapter is all about sleep — specifically, about your children and how *they* sleep. For you, all hope is lost — at least until your kids are grown and living on their own.

Helping your children get a good night's sleep is imperative for them to function well. As the one in charge, you need to provide the structure for your children's good sleep habits.

Ensuring That Kids Get Enough Zzzs

Kids need different amounts of sleep to feel alert, depending on their ages. As they mature, they gradually reduce the hours of sleep needed.

By 1 year, their bodies require just under 14 hours with two shorter nap times. By 2 years, you wrestle your active toddler down for about 13 hours, which includes only one nap.

Kids need slightly less sleep each year. During elementary grades, expect your sleepyhead to zone out for about 10 hours, compared with your grownup needs of 8¼ hours.

 Teenagers should have at least 9¼ hours of sleep, but their bodies turn weird at puberty. Their body clock shifts, which creates havoc on them and the family schedule. Suddenly, their hormones tell them to stay up later and sleep later. Even when they turn out the lights at 9:30 to get their normal nine hours of sleep, they may lie staring at the ceiling (and have to rush to make it to school on time). Adolescents aren't all lazy. Many are just sleep deprived.

Getting enough sleep translates to academic achievement

Research supports the strong connection between enough sleep and academic achievement. Improvements with more sleep have been so noticeable that Minneapolis Public Schools now juggle starting times to accommodate recommended sleep schedules: By opening school later in middle and high schools, the district reports increases in attendance, alertness, and overall academic achievement — all this without threats of whips, detention, or expensive tutors!

Push for later starting times for junior high and high school students. Contact your school's PTO/PTA or the principal to get the idea rolling. If the school isn't interested, write letters to your local newspapers and other media outlets. At the very least, all the teens in the neighborhood will be your friend, but keep in mind that research does support your stance.

You know your child — whether a preschooler or high-schooler — needs more sleep when she

- Finds concentrating and remembering difficult
- Looks tired (puffy or red eyes, sallow skin color, disheveled) — at least more than normal
- Acts irritable (more than usual)
- Tends to make mistakes or seems clumsier
- Seems slower acting and less creative
- Loses interest in activities or social life
- Catches more colds or other bugs
- Falls asleep in class

Making Strategic Bedtime Plans

The Golden Rule when putting your children to bed, regardless of their ages, is this: *They must be sleepy.* Trying to put them to bed when they're not tired is a fruitless effort. Your kids more than likely fight bedtime anyway.

Before you actually try to put your children to bed, work up to bedtime. That means helping your kids to feel sleepy. You can accomplish this task by following these steps:

1 Play with your child in the afternoon or early evening; encourage lots of activity.

This physical activity is not only good for kids, but it also makes them more ready for bed. Basically, you're trying to wear them out late in the day so they're ready to sleep at night.

2 Offer your child a snack.

Feeding your kids before they go to bed makes them more likely to sleep longer and not wake up in the middle of the night wanting food. Snacktime also starts the process of calming down your children. (Keep in mind, though, that snacking is an optional stage, because some kids won't need a snack before going to bed. That's perfectly okay.)

Good evening snacks are warm bowls of soup or a warm grilled-cheese sandwich. Feeding your children something with *substance* gives them a full, comfy feeling, which helps make them feel sleepy. Feed them sweets, however, at your own peril.

3 Give your child a bath.

It should be a calm, relaxing time — you don't want to start a water fight that'll get kids pumped up and ready to go some more.

4 Have a quiet time to calm your child down.

Turn off the television, put on some soothing music (or just have it quiet), and grab a good book to read to your kids. When they're too young to sit and really listen, just go through the book and point out the pictures, or make up your own stories as you go along.

Remember: Giving your kids enough time to quiet down is important. The amount of time required depends on your children. For some, it may be only 15 minutes. For others, it may be an hour. That's why snacktime and bathtime also need to be a part of the calming phase for your kids.

5 Put your child to bed, turn off the light, and leave.

After all your preparation is done, tuck her into bed, kiss her goodnight, turn on the nightlight, *and leave.* It's that simple. (If it's not that simple for you, see the following section.)

This ritual needs to be followed every night. Don't feel bad, though, when you find it's too late for the bath or story. You've probably done something else to fill in that time anyway. But try to stick to your schedule as much as possible. When your kids are used to it, they'll fall asleep more easily than when they're all wound up and pumped full of sugar with action/adventure shows running through their heads.

Troubleshooting Sleep Behaviors That Need to Change

An example of a sleep behavior that needs to change is when your child wakes up more during the night than you can tolerate. For some parents, that's five times a night; for others, it's only once. If your child wakes up once a night and you don't have a problem with that, then your family doesn't have a sleep problem.

 Parents need to set realistic expectations. Just because many books say that, starting at about 6 months, children should sleep 12 hours a night without waking up and should be able to fall asleep without any help, that doesn't mean it's the reality for most parents. Most children (and therefore parents) struggle with nighttime waking and falling asleep at some point during childhood. When evaluating your child's sleep situation, make sure that you're being realistic and not holding your child up to an ideal that often doesn't exist.

Creating a family bed

Many families deal with nighttime waking by creating a *family bed*, meaning the parents and children sleep together. People who like the idea of sleeping with their kids all agree that it's a great time to bond and spend time with their children. They love the idea of cuddling, and besides, parents have been sleeping with their babies for thousands of years.

On the other hand, people who disagree with the idea think it's a bad habit to start. They say it allows neither the children nor the parents to sleep well. They say kids need to learn independence, and having their own bed is the first step toward that independence. A safety issue is also involved: You have to be careful not to roll over on a small child or use big pillows and comforters that can smother him.

 If creating a family bed is a solution that's right for you, be sure to keep your children safe. For safety guidelines, check out www.parentsplace.com (search for "sleeping" to find several informative articles on the topic) or pick up a copy of *The No-Cry Sleep Solution* by Elizabeth Pantley.

Like most situations in parenting, there's always room for compromise, even within the family bed debate. A couple of compromises follow:

❀ Create a place in your room, but not in your bed, for the child to sleep.

❀ Welcome your child into your bed for those times when he doesn't feel well and is having a hard time falling asleep. Let him fall asleep next to you but then take him to his own bed.

Other solutions for kids who wake up during the night

Many times kids may sound like they're awake when they really aren't fully awake. Don't be tempted to run into their rooms to comfort your children. All you'd really be doing is waking them up. They'll go back to sleep on their own.

Try standing outside the bedroom door or just peeking in. If they're still in bed, all is well. If they're standing in their room crying, that means something different.

When a child actually gets up, walks out of her room and into yours, and then taps you on the shoulder, you know she's definitely awake. Persistence on your part is key here. Don't be tempted to stay up and play (you'd be starting a bad habit). Take her to go potty, give her a drink, and then escort her back to bed. If she gets right up, take her again. Don't give in no matter how tired you are. She has to learn that 3 o'clock in the morning is not a time to get up and watch TV. It's a time for sleep.

Although you may have to endure several nights of crying and whining, *you'll* stop soon enough. This situation is one where you'll have to consistently take your kids to bed. Not to worry, though. They'll eventually grow out of it.

Here are some other solutions to consider:

❋ If your children routinely wake up and just want something to drink, leave a cup of water by their beds.

❋ When your children actually wake up, try not to pick them up or have them walk. Doing so gives them the false hope that they get to play for a while — which you know not to be true — and it wakes them up even more.

Changing habits that *you* started

Although it seems that some children are born good sleepers and others need a lot more assistance, many sleeping problems begin with habits that you develop with your newborn — habits that *you* start. In fact, most sleeping problems develop during the first year of life. So be aware that your habit is the one that needs to be broken. Your child is logically expecting you to continue whatever bedtime habit you were in before. In her little world, you're the one who's behaving illogically, so she'll put up a fight.

That said, if you're trying to get rid of certain bedtime habits and creating a family bed isn't right for you, try a different approach. Start by explaining what you're going to do. "Daddy needs to be sure that you're in bed by 8 o'clock. I know that Daddy let you stay up later before, but then I noticed

that you get really cranky in the morning. So, I'm guessing that you need more sleep."

When they argue, listen to their protestations but continue reinforcing your position: "But what can I do so that you aren't cranky in the morning?" It also helps when you reinforce your position as long before bedtime as possible. Trying to explain your position when your kids are already in bed invites them to talk and become excited, which is counterproductive.

Follow the same rules of preparing your children for bed that are described in the earlier section "Making Strategic Bedtime Plans." Then, when it's time for them to go to sleep, kiss them goodnight and leave the room. They may or may not fuss for a while.

 After you leave the room, listen carefully. Are your children fussing (whining, whimpering), or are they screaming bloody murder? There's a difference. *Fussing* means only that your child isn't really happy with the situation but can live with it for a while. *Screaming bloody murder* means you need to go in and help out a little.

If you're dealing with the latter, go in and comfort your child and then leave again. (*Comforting* means laying your child back down and stroking her hair for a few minutes. Don't pick her up, because she'll be *really* mad when you put her down again.) Wait a little longer before you go in the next time. Gradually add to the time that you wait before going back in and remind your child that she just has to be in bed. If she wants to just lie there, that's fine, but she must be in bed. If she's sleepy, she'll stop fighting it and go to sleep.

You'll probably need to take the time to wean your child from your old sleeping ritual by combining it with leaving while she's still awake. For example, if you've developed the habit of patting your child on the back while she falls asleep, gradually reduce the amount of time that you pat her back. Be prepared to go back into the room and pat some more if she cries, but then leave after a few minutes. Gradually increase the amount of time that you're gone and decrease the amount of time that you stay in the room. This weaning process won't happen overnight. You've developed a habit that your child likes, and she isn't going to part with it willingly.

Here are a couple more tips:

* **Explain bedtime to your children.** Let them know that it's coming. Give them warnings: "Thirty minutes to bedtime!" then "15 minutes," then "10 minutes," then "5," then "1," and then a countdown of "10, 9, 8, 7, 6, 5, 4, 3, 2, 1." Kids feel comfortable when they know what to expect. Setting a timer can also be very helpful. Older kids can set the timer for the designated amount of time and, when it rings, they know it's time to go to bed.

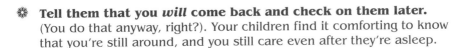
✿ **Tell them that you _will_ come back and check on them later.**
(You do that anyway, right?). Your children find it comforting to know
that you're still around, and you still care even after they're asleep.

Remember: Putting your children to bed every night and keeping them
there isn't always going to go smoothly. If every night seems to be a struggle, review your nighttime ritual to see whether you or your children are
doing something that makes going to bed even harder. Ask these
questions:

✿ Are they really tired, or do you just think they should go to bed?

✿ Are they getting too many sweets or too much caffeine before bed?

✿ Are they getting too much stimulation right before bedtime?

✿ Is there too much noise outside the bedroom?

✿ Does your child have a fear that she isn't talking about?

✿ How's the room temperature?

Handling Naps

Napping schedules really depend on the child. Some kids are nappers,
some aren't. Newborns nap all the time. But by the time children reach age
3 or 4, they may be taking only one nap a day or simply lying down with a
book to rest. Some kids may want a nap until they're 5 or 6. Some kids
start fighting naps at age 2. You'll have to determine what your children
need as they grow up.

 Don't worry about the amount of sleep that your children are getting. They'll
sleep as much as they need to. But when afternoon naps are getting longer
and your children are going to bed later and later at night, you may want to
start waking them up earlier from their afternoon naps. You don't want to
have to stay up until midnight because your toddler's nap was too long and
now she isn't tired.

Try keeping your children on a daily schedule (or routine) for naps. Your
children will go down easier knowing that naptime comes after lunch and a
story, for example.

If your children don't seem to want to take a nap, consider these factors:

✿ **Did you get them ready for a nap?** Getting them ready means
calm, quiet activities. Or did you just take them off the trampoline
to put them to bed?

✿ **Did you check for dirty diapers, if applicable?**

❀ **Is the room contributing to a nap?** Make the room quiet, with neither bright lights nor piles of toys in bed, not too hot or too cold, but just right.

❀ **Is it naptime?** If it isn't, have your children displayed signs of needing a nap, such as being cranky, rubbing their eyes, and whining? Perhaps they became overexcited and are too wound up for a nap. You'll have to take time to wind them back down so they can rest.

❀ **Are your children getting too old for naps?** Perhaps your children are reaching the age — which varies from child to child — when they won't go to sleep, but they still need to lie down with a book and rest.

Chapter 8

Diapers, Hit the Road

Potty training is not all that hard. The trick is not to start too early or have the attitude "As of today — as God is my witness — my child is going to learn to use the potty."

Your child has to be physically and emotionally ready to use the potty because no matter how much *you* want it to happen, using the potty is really up to your child. In addition, you need to have a plan for potty training. This chapter helps you determine whether your child is ready and provides you with that plan.

In This Chapter

☺ Looking for signs that your child is ready for potty training

☺ Figuring out the best time to train your child

☺ Preparing your child in advance of the training

☺ Following a four-step potty-training plan

Recognizing the Signs of Readiness

If you can successfully pin down the time when your child is really ready for potty training — typically from 18 to 24 months old — you enhance your chances of helping him succeed by 75 percent. Between 18 months and 3 years, most children reach the point of muscle control that makes self-regulation possible. So when that is apparent, along with an interest in using the potty and other strong indicators, go for it.

Here are some signs of readiness (items with an asterisk at the end are musts for potty-training success):

❀ Stays dry for at least two hours*

❀ Gets bummed by wet or messy diapers*

❀ Knows potty lingo (the meaning of *wet, dry, pee, poop* or *BM, messy* or *dirty, clean,* and *bottom*)*

❋ Likes to please*

❋ Imitates and follows simple instructions*

❋ Asks for diaper changes

❋ Likes things in the proper place

From your child's point of view, using the toilet constitutes multitasking taken to a whole new and scary level. He needs certain skills and a certain level of maturity to tackle the project successfully. For successful potty training, a toddler should have impulse control, improved motor skills, and a desire for autonomy. Plus, he must be packing several key physical skills:

❋ The ability to signal the need to go to the potty

❋ The ability to walk

❋ The ability to undress by himself

❋ The ability to get onto the potty

❋ The ability to control his sphincter

And you must consider these little follow-ups:

❋ Pulling off the right amount of toilet paper

❋ Wiping properly

❋ Disposing of the toilet paper

❋ Flushing

❋ Washing up

In addition, look for these significant clues:

❋ Your child urinates a large amount at one time.

❋ His bowel movements are well formed and fairly regular.

And to make things even more complex, he needs that all-important, but sometimes elusive, willingness to cooperate.

You need to be aware that your child's need-to-go sensation isn't fully developed when he starts potty training. It develops during the process. He's used to going in his diaper as a matter of course, so getting to the point where he can tell you that he needs to go potty before doing his business in his diaper takes some practice. And know that the ability to inhibit muscle contractions following the first urge to urinate varies greatly from child to child.

Choosing the Right Time to Potty Train

Slot on your calendar a nice, calm weekend for potty training when you'll have ample time to focus. At the outset, your child will need lots of attention and help, and you'll want to provide exactly that.

 Spring and summer are quintessential potty-training start-up times simply because a child wears fewer clothes in warm weather. And the ones she does have on will be light and scanty: loose shorts, tiny dresses, not much to fool with.

But just like you'd do if starting potty training in the summer or spring, you can choose an easygoing, laid-back weekend in the fall or winter for kicking off the process. Just make sure that the spot you use for the potty chair is warm and comfy, and have on hand a good supply of cozy, loose clothes that your child won't mind pulling down even though it's cold outside.

Certain kinds of moments stir up a kid too much for her to be able to learn new tricks. The following should probably be labeled "no go" times for starting up potty training:

❋ If you've just gotten a divorce or separated from your mate, or if the family is going through heavy-duty conflict.

❋ If you've just moved.

❋ The month after the arrival of a new baby or the adoption of an older child.

❋ If you've just gotten married and the new stepparent is bringing in a slew of stepsiblings.

❋ When your toddler moves from her baby bed to a twin bed. Same goes for when she's weaning from breast or bottle to the cup.

❋ A change in caregivers.

❋ When your child is in an overall moody frame of mind.

Prepping for Potty Training Weekend

If you're slow and methodical in your approach to potty training, expect to see an amazing degree of cooperation. Go into it without planning, and you can look for things to erupt in chaos.

Start by letting your potty-trainee watch you and other family members use the toilet so that he can check it out firsthand. In childcare settings, he'll see other kids using the potty, which will pique his interest; plus, the peer pressure helps get your child mentally ready. Also start letting your little one practice clothed potty-sits and invite him to observe how you dispose of diaper contents.

Let your child watch you use the toilet

A terrific setup for potty training is letting your child watch you, your mate, and siblings use the toilet. (If possible, have your child focus on same-sex folks.) That way, the child gets to see how people use the bathroom and why they do what they do.

Avoid the biggest mistake parents make in role modeling toilet use, which is rushing through it. We all lead such hurry-up lives, but your child will do much better if you're very methodical, allowing plenty of time for him to absorb all the moves.

Go snail-slow when you give verbal instructions. You have to allow time for your child to take in the information. Carefully explain each step:

- **Getting clothes off and climbing on the potty.** Say, "Watch how I pull down my pants, and let's see you try it, too." That should get him rolling. "Now, let's see you climb onto the potty, just for fun."

- **Doing potty business.** Tell him that when you or his sister sits on the potty, both of you expect some poop or pee to come out. "And when you start using the potty, that's where your poop or pee goes when you do your business."

- **Wiping.** Demonstrate how to tear off some toilet paper and wipe clean. "You try to get just a small amount because too much clogs up the toilet." Talk about proper wiping but don't overload him with information right now.

- **Flushing.** The basics of flushing may seem simple to you, but that's not the case for your small fry. And what if your toddler latches onto toilet flushing as his new best hobby? That's a normal response to a fun skill, but waste no time in pointing out that toilets aren't toys; they are types of bathroom equipment meant to be used correctly.

- **Washing up.** Show how to wash up thoroughly afterward. Again, make it a methodical explanation. Using soap and warm water, show your child how he can gauge whether he is washing long enough: "You have to sing the 'Happy Birthday' song all the way through." When he's only 2 years old, you'll be the one singing the song, but later, he will be able to do this.

Let your child practice clothed potty-sits

Letting your child sit on the potty while he is wearing clothes is key to getting him used to the feel of a potty chair (see Figure 8-1) or the adapter atop an adult toilet (see Figure 8-2).

Figure 8-1: An on-the-floor potty chair is easy for kids to sit down on but has to be emptied.

Figure 8-2: A toilet-topper doesn't have to be emptied, but your kid will need help getting up.

☺ ☺

During these clothed potty-sits, talk about Potty Training Weekend that's coming up and explain that when the weekend arrives, he'll start out by using the potty without his clothes on. Tell him that he'll be allowed to run around naked and that he'll be getting used to the potty chair. Eventually, when he's pottying in it, he'll graduate to his big-boy underpants.

✻ **Get him comfy with the chair.** Later on, you'll probably still hear complaints like "it's cold." But it'll help that his clothing-clad rear end has already been introduced to the potty chair.

✻ **Encourage curiosity as he practices the clothed potty-sits.** If he studies how the chair is made, takes it apart, or picks it up and puts it on his head, that's all part of the process.

✻ **Don't press the issue if he gets bored with sitting or resists.** Do not cajole or persuade. Be casual. Be jaunty.

✻ **Promote playfulness.** Some kids like to cart the potty chair around the house and let their toys and animals try using it. The more familiar and comfortable he gets with his chair, the more likely he will adapt to using it with relative ease.

Let your child watch you dispose of diaper contents

Make a point of having your child watch you empty his diaper contents into the bowl of his new potty chair. "Why?" he may ask. You say, "Because this is where poop is supposed to go." He'll probably ask why one more time after that. Your answer: "Remember how we've talked about things having places? You like to put your toys in the toy box, right? Well, we like to put poop and pee in the toilet because that's where they go. Then we flush it away." Tell him that this is what his siblings do with their pee and poop, and so do his aunt and uncle, you, lots of grownup people, and big kids.

Your child may react to this in a variety of ways. Some kids are fascinated by the flushing and the poop disappearing act. Others show no interest at all. The worrywarts may be upset by seeing the poop get flushed away. If flushing makes your child anxious, wait to flush until he leaves the room — or leave the poop in the toilet for a while.

Potty Training Weekend

The big weekend has arrived. In this one memorable weekend, your little star will learn the steps of potty use. She's going to make her way through the steps of helping a doll use the potty, sitting on the potty every hour and managing the tissue-pull, the wipe, and the wash-up, setting up her progress chart, and moving up to training pants.

☺ ☺ ☺ ☺ ☺ ☺ ☺ ☺ ☹ ☺ ☺ ☹ ☺ ☺ ☹ ☺ ☺ ☺ ☹ ☺

During Potty Training Weekend, you, the coach, will lead your child to the potty often, praise her efforts and successes, breeze through accidents, and keep her needs first. You'll also make sure that the kid is super-charged. Tell her, "We'll have a great Potty Training Weekend, and you'll be leaving diapers behind after you learn how big kids pee and poop in the toilet."

Prepping your child and feeding for success

Point out where the potty chair is and explain that you'll help her get situated when it's time to get on it. Put her in her birthday suit. Your goal is to do everything you can to simplify her sprint from the urge to pee or poop to going in the potty.

To help improve her chances of being successful, feed her foods that keep her elimination processes flowing freely. Keep the water and juice flowing, too. To help make sure that your child drinks a lot, you may want to hand out some tasty salty snacks and also feed her stool-softening foods, such as brown rice; dried fruits; fiber breakfast bars; fresh fruits such as apricots, berries, grapes, and plums; prune juice; veggies; and whole-grain breads and cereals. And try to avoid foods that tend to constipate, such as cheese, excessive milk, pasta, and white bread.

Tell your child about the digestive process: She eats food and drinks liquids, and they travel down to her tummy where most of it fuels her body so she's able to run, dance, and climb. The rest of the food and drink — the part that she doesn't need — leaves her body and goes into her diapers, and now she's learning to put it directly into the potty. Poop represents the leftovers from food, and pee, leftovers from things she drank.

Let her know that she's in control of this: "Sweetie, you're the one making your poop and the pee. And you're the one who can decide where it goes and what to do with it."

Step 1: Helping a doll use the potty

A fairly effective way to get your child to focus on learning potty stuff is to have her teach a doll or stuffed animal (or even an action figure if your child prefers) how to use the potty. The first thing you do when you're ready to model potty-training practices with the doll is ask your trainee to go get a pair of her brand-new training pants and put them on the doll. Then help her take the doll through its paces:

1 **Pull the doll's pants down.**

2 **Put the doll on the potty chair.**

3   Encourage the doll to pee (and have it actually do so if it's a doll that wets).

4   Praise the doll (even if you're just pretending it peed) and talk about how fun that was.

5   Get your toddler to help with wiping the doll's behind, dumping the doll's pee and poop into the big toilet, and washing the doll's hands (unless the doll isn't supposed to get wet).

Step 2: Sitting on the potty

The next step is getting your child to sit on the potty after training the doll. Put the doll aside and ask your child to take the doll's place on the potty. Encourage the whole routine: pulling down the training pants, sitting on the potty, and waiting.

In addition, show her how to wipe carefully (front to back) and help your child learn how to thoroughly wash her hands. But don't put too much focus on getting this part perfect at the get-go because she's undoubtedly going to have enough trouble remembering to key into the feel of needing to poop and pee and making it to the chair in time.

Your goal is to help her learn to listen to her body. Explain the signs. And be sure to ask your child to cue you when she needs to go potty. But more often, you'll be escorting her to the potty for an *hourly* potty-sit. Keep your child on a routine. And just as you do when housetraining a puppy, take her to the bathroom shortly after meals.

 Even though you want to encourage many potty-sits, don't pressure your child. Enthuse over what happens — whether she actually goes potty or not.

In addition, any time she tells you "I peed" or "I pooped," even though she did it in her diaper or underpants, praise her like crazy for telling you. Often, that leads to a fabulous next step — she'll tell you *before* something happens.

 Too many parents stick a kid on the chair and run away to do other things. During Potty Training Weekend, you absolutely have to make a big impression, and that takes ample time and friendly hovering.

Step 3: Setting up a success chart

Help your child set up a star or sticker success chart. Make a big deal of how neat it will be when she gets sticker or star rewards that she can put

on her success chart. Little kids love stickers and stars, and this kind of reward setup can be very motivating.

Follow up any instance of successful peeing or pooping in the potty — or good tries — with the reward: a sticker or star on her chart. Of course, continue to give lots of verbal praise, too.

Stay positive no matter how grumpy she gets. If she says, "I don't want a star chart! I hate this!" turn her attention away from the potty to some fun game. Don't get into a lecture on why she has to learn the potty, like it or not. **Remember:** A toddler will forget her stubborn stand against almost anything in 30 minutes or less. Little-kid grudges evaporate quickly.

Step 4: Switching to training pants

If your toddler gets the general idea of how to use the potty chair for peeing and pooping, move her into training pants during Potty Training Weekend. Do so for sure if you see your child showing good control of urination and bowel movements.

Look for a string of ten or so potty successes to tell you she's ready for training pants. Then you can safely discontinue diapers. You want her to wear these training pants every day, even though three months may pass before she gets the merit badge that says "accident-free." Your signal to switch your child into *regular* underwear is her showing that she can use the potty chair regularly. Her reward: She gets to wear the "graduation" undies and save training pants for sleep time. Also, she will interpret this as a sign of your trust in her — she's a big kid!

 If your child puts on training pants by the end of Potty Training Weekend, she may well be potty trained for daytime in six or seven weeks. Nights take longer, so continue to use the training pants at night because that extra absorbency will make bedwetting much less embarrassing. But do be ready for plenty of setbacks and accidents — they're just normal parts of the process. Be casual about the accidents, not overly concerned. You need to guide and lead, not punish and scold.

 If you get so frustrated by accidents that you stick your child back in diapers, she's going to be bummed. There she was, gliding along, not always smoothly but fairly proud of herself, wearing big-kid underpants, when you jerked her progress symbols right off of her. If your child were more verbal, she'd say to you, "Tell me what's going on here. Am I bad because I have accidents that I can't really help? I feel like you're telling me I'm a naughty girl when you take my new pants away from me. But I'm doing my best." She's confused, and this is no time for mixed messages. Stick with the upgrade pants.

Ways to Keep Potty Training Working

Keeping your focus goes a long way toward preventing potty training from becoming an extended, on-again-off-again ordeal. When your toddler has shown some success and is regularly sitting on the potty several times a day, you can chalk it up as a trend. Now he is more likely to go in the potty than his diaper.

To keep potty training working, remember to pull out all the stops on reinforcing good stuff. And continue to deal with accidents with a lilt in your voice and by heaping affection on your child even though he's still having the accidents.

In addition, know that there will be times when you will probably need to step back and take a deep breath. Rein yourself in. You must remember not to drive your child wacko.

 Hard as it is to remember, keep chanting that learning to use the potty is your little one's challenge, not yours. You can assist, cheer on, and support. But only your child can make it happen and turn it into a habit.

Part 3

Guiding Your Child through the Years

Raising your child to be a well balanced, confident, responsible, and independent person is what the chapters in this part are all about. These chapters contain guidelines, suggestions, and tips you can use to help your child develop into a person you'll be proud to know.

In this part, you find out why kids act the way they do at certain ages and how to respond to and deal with them. You get advice on how to handle tough times — when your kids choose not to follow the rules and boundaries you've established, when your kids suffer the loss of a parent through death or divorce, or when your kids have to move to a new school. You receive guidelines and suggestions for dealing with common family matters, such as sibling rivalry and single parenting. You look at ways to get help — from your spouse, role models, and childcare providers. And you get advice on instilling good social skills and manners.

Chapter 9

What's Going On Upstairs: Your Child's Emotional Development

Is your toddler going through that stage where he's afraid of scary things? Does your teenage son seem to be ignoring you lately? How about your teenage daughter? Does she need a lot of encouragement at this awkward stage of her life? You want to meet the needs of your children at whatever age or stage they're at, but doing so can become a little overwhelming at times.

This chapter explains what's going on upstairs — why kids act the way they do at certain ages. And it provides some helpful tips for being the best parent you can possibly be to your kids, because when you understand your kids' ages and stages, you'll know how to react to and deal with them.

The Toddler/Preschooler Stage

If you think a break is in order after bringing up baby, just wait. You have your work cut out for you now. Raising toddlers and preschoolers is a full-time job.

What you can expect

Just when you get a handle on raising your child, you get blindsided by temper tantrums, rampant "no's," rebelliousness, bossy pickiness, and — the worst — limp body drops.

A toddler wants what she wants *now!* Stamp your foot for emphasis, and you're pretty much behaving like your toddler. In order for her to let you know she's not a baby anymore, she feels compelled to shout the message from rooftops, or the middle of the grocery store floor, whichever is more convenient. In other words, your toddler asserts her growing independence any way she can, but because a toddler's options for expression are limited, you get the screaming, demanding, and contrary foot-stamping.

There's more. Welcome to the I-can-do-it-myself (or me-do-it) stage. This is the age of the

- ❀ Quick-change artist or, if you're really lucky, outdoor stripper

- ❀ Mechanical wizard who unfastens the car seat belt while you're zooming along the expressway

- ❀ Self-help queen who pours her own juice, spilling enough to wash the table and create a wading pool on the floor for the dog

- ❀ Shopper helper who drops scores of unwanted but colorful items into your shopping cart

- ❀ Fashion plate who goes to restaurants only if she's wearing her tutu, red boots, and 10-gallon hat

Kids this age naturally want to do everything for themselves, even when they aren't always successful. And they want to do what you do because they think being an adult has more perks than being a kid. (Little do they know what's ahead!)

What you can do to help

First, relax. Believe it or not, the way you know your child is progressing is because these uproars occur. Your child rebels, for example, because she wants more to life. She's curious. She's talkative. She has new interests. She's becoming her own person.

Some experts call this tumultuous toddlerhood *first adolescence.* This is your child's passage — for some, kicking and screaming — from babyhood into childhood. (Don't confuse this time with the teenage years, which have been called *second adolescence.*)

With tantrums

To handle all the foot-stamping, screaming, and demanding, consider which rules are really important for your child to learn. Yes, rules. Even though your tot bucks you every step, she really wants the comfort of your guiding parameters. She needs boundaries, as all children do, to feel secure and safe, knowing that someone else is in control and keeping her

little life on a predictable, even course. Your little one needs rules to discover more about herself and about how to be with others.

The trick is to provide rules that are like Goldilocks and the Three Bears — not so overbearing that you stifle her feelings of self-worth, not so freeform that she can't grasp how to function, but just right. She needs guidelines for acting so that others can stand to be around her, but she can still have some wiggle room to develop her weird-and-wacky or quiet-and-serious personality.

Be sure you follow your just-right rules consistently, or your sweetie won't know which direction to go. By *consistent,* I mean providing the exact same response handled in the same way every time your child flops on the grocery store floor and wails, no matter how stressed you are one time versus the next. Your child sees flip-flopping as a real weak spot in your character, and one to be exploited. She understands that the unacceptable will eventually be permitted if she continues to badger you long enough, so be vigilant.

If you'd like detailed info about setting boundaries, being consistent, following through, and managing behavior, check out Chapters 3 and 4 of this book. They're dedicated to those very subjects.

With me-do-it madness

To handle the I-can-do-it-myself stage, the first thing you should consider is this: Do you want to discourage her unique behavior so that you don't risk being labeled the most eccentric family in the neighborhood? No way! Any neighbor who doesn't understand the toddler desire for autonomy doesn't know toddlers — or isn't much fun with them.

The I-can-do-it-myself stage is the beginning of the drive, willingness to work, and optimism identified as characteristics of smarter kids. Properly managed, this stage helps her budding self-image turn into a can-do approach later in life.

So what are you supposed to do when you're out of time and/or your child dawdles over tasks you'd rather finish yourself quickly? Do you have a choice when your child insists on performing an activity that's far too difficult for her? Here are some not-so-foolproof options to try:

❋ **Allow your child to tackle a difficult job, but stay close by.** If you see frustration building, ask whether she wants help. If the stars line up, she may permit your intervention, the task will be completed, and all will be well in Toddlerland.

❀ **Distract your child with a more pleasant assignment so that you can handle the task at hand.** For example, offer your tot a chance to read a favorite book or hold her prized teddy while you tie her shoes.

❀ **Break down the tasks involved in what your child wants to accomplish.** Assign an appropriate task to her, and you do the hard stuff. Make sure your child knows that her part of the job is very important. For example, "Let's pour the juice together. You hold the cup very still, the hard part. I'll pour from the container."

❀ **Take the offending article along with you, if you're in a rush.** This gives you some extra time to work out a plan, one where you can complete the job without a violent response. There's no law that says your child has to wear shoes into the car or have a buttoned sweater before leaving the house.

❀ **Arrange small jobs your child can do to work alongside you before a struggle develops.** Kids just want to play grownup. Give your youngster a dust rag. Buy her a pretend rug sweeper or small snow shovel or rake. Ask for her assistance making beds and setting the table. If you're brave and available for close supervision, give your child a few minutes of pushing the real vacuum, spraying the windows with cleaner, or smushing the polish on the table.

Remember: Don't expect perfection. And whatever you do, never redo anything your child has just done. Nothing deflates your child more than seeing someone adjust, pick at, or otherwise change something she worked so hard on. And that goes for children of any age and spouses, for that matter. If the job has to be done a certain way, don't give it to anyone else to do. Keep it to yourself and assign a more workable but similar task for your child to do by your side. "Daddy slices the roast. But you can arrange the parsley on the serving platter."

❀ **Assign responsibilities your child can handle,** such as watching the baby on the rug or picking up toys. These seemingly little jobs give your child a chance to try out what being grownup is like.

❀ **Celebrate minor and major accomplishments.** Whoop and holler over staying dry at night, riding a tricycle for the first time, or putting on a coat like a big kid.

❀ **Point out how important certain objects are,** such as nails that hold furniture and walls together or tiny serving spoons for ice cream. This gives your child the message that she is important, too, even though she's little.

The School-Age Stage

If you have a child in the 5- to 12-year-old bracket, you're facing a different problem every week.

What you can expect

One week your 8-year-old may suddenly become afraid of the dark or bullies at the bus stop, and the next week, your lovely, mature daughter may decide to throw a tantrum at the mall. Yes, although toddlers are often the tantrum-throwing culprits, older children sometimes throw them, too.

And preteens, the older group of the school-age stage, start itching for greater independence. Because independence is not theirs for the asking yet, they experiment within their limited boundaries. Sometimes, experimentation takes the form of petty theft, pranks, teasing, sneaking out of the house, and other behaviors that test your response. What they do can be pretty scary.

 Why do preteens experiment so much? Because kids this age are grappling with defining who they are while trying to fit in — two important motivations for separating from you.

Toward the end of this stage, bodies change in outwardly obvious ways, too. Cliques form, which can be agony for those outside the group. Insiders pick on outsiders as a way to bolster their own forming psyches. Remember back to the preteen years yourself. These are tough times, socially and emotionally.

What you can do to help

Take all fears seriously. Never disregard them as insignificant. Sympathize with the child and offer a way out. For example, if your 7-year-old is afraid of the dark, take him with you to purchase a nightlight. Or if your child is afraid of a bully, empower him with smart alternatives so that the same situation doesn't happen again (see the nearby "Beating back bullies" sidebar for suggestions).

As for those preteen antics, your job as the parent during this stage is to set reasonable boundaries and stick to the rules you've set. Preteens may want more independence, but your job is to keep them safe by providing structure and clear expectations. Stick to the household rules and their consequences unwaveringly. Keep lines of communication open. And act fairly. Do these things, and you'll sail through this stage quicker than you can say, "Oh my goodness, a teenager lives in this house!"

 When your children reach the age of 10 or so, sit them down and have a frank discussion about drugs and alcohol. Many parents think that they can wait until their kids become teenagers to tackle these subjects, but that's not the case. Kids are introduced to drugs and alcohol in elementary school and junior high, so you need to face this potential problem head on.

Beating back bullies

Nothing brings out the tiger in you more than someone bullying your kid. But resist the urge to rush in and save your child. Better to empower your child with smart alternatives so that the same situation doesn't happen again.

* **Get the facts before attempting any action.** Find out your child's role in this unwanted relationship. Is there something your child does to bug the bully? What has your child tried already? What were the results?

* **Talk with your child if you discover that he causes the problem.** Yes, your darling is as capable of threatening others as the next kid. So identify the reason for any undesirable behavior. Impress upon your child that bullying or joining in bullying is wrong. Offer healthy ways to handle aggression and activities to build confidence so that he won't feel the need to bully anyone else.

* **Let your child try to handle the bully alone at first.** Offer these suggestions to your child: Confront the bully and ask why the incidents occur. Stay nonchalant, because bullies want to get a rise out of their victims and embarrass them. Inform the bully in a firm voice that this type of behavior must end, because bullies choose to bother kids they don't think will challenge them. If talking doesn't work, avoid the bully, steer clear of bathrooms or secluded places, and take alternate routes to school, a job, or the playground. Tell an adult at school, because teachers and administrators have the responsibility to provide a safe place to learn. (Emphasize that this isn't tattling. Your child is actually helping other kids whom the bully may hurt.)

* **Contact the child's parents yourself, should your child's efforts fail.** But understand that parents may be of little help. Chances are a troubled child comes from a troubled family.

* **Talk with school personnel.** Go as high as you need, even to the superintendent, to get results. If nothing seems to work or a large group bullies your child, you may want to consider transferring your child to another school.

* **Instill in your child the confidence to ward off bullies.** Kids who feel confident are more apt to compromise and negotiate without feeling they are losing face in front of other kids, which is what a bully wants.

The Teenage Stage

By the teenage years, your child turns into another type of animal altogether. Your teen pushes you away even farther as he draws you nearer. He wants to become his own person yet still seeks your approval. And then car keys, late-night outings, and expanding financial needs enter the picture.

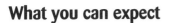
What you can expect

In trying to wade into adult waters, your teen may

❁ **Test the child rules that have kept your family balanced for years.** Your older child is trying to come up with a smart system of behaviors and philosophies that work for him.

❁ **Feel a strong need to separate from you.** In fact, the more stringent you are, the more your teen rebels. He figures the only way to attain independence is to reject you and everything you hold dear. *Remember:* Teens also respect individuality and being different, which is weird considering most dress like clones. Prepare for your child to find expression of this individuality in different behavior, music, hairstyle, dress, and possibly a tattoo or a piercing or two. All this trouble arrives because he now finds the family routine stifling. You may think he's thrown all his marbles out the window. He hasn't. He's just rebelling.

❁ **Criticize, avoid, or otherwise view you as the source of his embarrassment and roadblock to living life.** You are the parent of a teen. Therefore, you know nothing short of Neanderthal wisdom, if any wisdom at all.

❁ **Exhibit wild mood swings.** He suddenly balks at a request you've made many times before, gives you a bear hug 30 minutes later, or storms out of the house with little provocation. Turbulence is from teen hormones, and boys as well as girls have high and low cyclical swings.

❁ **Look to friends for what's cool.** After all, your talk, dress, and value system are so retro (or whatever the term for old-fashioned is today).

❁ **Spend an inordinate amount of time communicating with friends, the known and unknown.** Besides e-mail and cell phones, teens use instant messaging (IM to your savvy teen) to fill their off-school time. In fact, multitasking is in, meaning your teen may watch television, send and receive e-mails, talk on the phone, and IM, all while convincing you he's studying.

❁ **Find greater need for space and privacy, which oddly enough gets expressed in large amounts of time spent communicating with peers electronically.** Expect to hear a lot of "Leave me alone" or see a closed bedroom door.

 Whatever gripes you have with the teenage stage, the transgressions aren't all your teen's fault. Adolescent hormones hit some kids like gangbusters and affect bodies, emotions, and actions (see Chapter 5 for specific body changes to expect at puberty).

What you can do to help

Here are some simple ways to help you help your teen through this tumultuous stage:

❀ **Respect your child's opinions and choices.** You don't always have to agree with your teen, and much of the time, you may wonder which planet he's from. But saying "I respect what you say" goes a long way toward building relationship bridges with adolescents. When you get his attention, you can make inroads into keeping him focused on achieving his best.

❀ **Offer explanations when you disagree.** You're not in the dark ages of your parents' youth, when folks emphasized "Because I said so" and expected rules to be followed blindly. Teens today are savvy, articulate, and brazen. If you want respect, you need to show a little yourself for his brain power. If you must lay down a law for your child's health and safety, offer an explanation of why that makes sense. Your child deserves as much.

❀ **Listen to your teen.** How many times have you heard, "You don't listen to me!" or "You don't get it!" Your teen just wants to be heard, acknowledged, and understood. Listen to his dreams no matter how unrealistic; you had dreams once, too. Your course of action is really quite simple. First, make yourself available. Then listen to what's important to your child, no matter how painful a topic. Listening, reflecting back what you've heard, and reacting to news in a non-judgmental way keeps your child confiding in you, which gives you a leg up on remaining a strong influence in his young life. In return, he listens to you and stays focused, sort of.

❀ **Trust your teen.** Trusting is like expecting high achievement. If you believe your child is trustworthy, he will live up to those expectations — well, most of the time. *Warning:* If your teen offers some way-out explanation for something that defies credibility, you have a right and obligation to investigate further, especially with unsafe behavior. But if the facts prove your child's case, be ready and willing to apologize.

❀ **Ask your child's opinion.** Your child claims to want more say in household matters, but his behavior sends the opposite message — that he isn't interested. Look beyond the negative behavior, surly responses, and closed doors and keep asking your child for ideas, alternatives, and opinions to show that you respect his judgment and actions. The more your child feels connected with you, your family, and what goes on at home, the less he'll be enticed by dangerous temptations from friends.

❀ **Find various ways to say positive statements and lots of "I love you."** Everyone needs to receive positive messages as often as possible, and so does your teen. Don't plant a wet smooch on his cheek in front of friends. But your child needs to know that you care as much and believe he's as capable as always, even though he's changing and may do some dumb stuff now and then.

❊ **Model wholesome behavior.** Teens throw your do-as-I-say-and-not-as-I-do actions back in your face. If you want a teen who doesn't drink and drive, swear, do drugs, or cover his body with tattoos, don't engage in these behaviors yourself. But if you want a teen who picks up a book now and then, works hard, and acts responsibly, show him how these activities are done.

❊ **Play fair.** Don't expect your teen to finish a ton of household chores knowing he has a debate to prepare for and a load of studying. Hire a babysitter for your younger child when your teen has a big dance on the same night you want to go out. Fairness counts big-time with teens, even if you think it's one-sided in your teen's favor. **Remember:** Let punishments fit the crimes. Grounding your teen for every infraction only makes him angry at you. If the problem is with the car, come up with a fair, car-related consequence to misbehavior. If completing math homework is the problem, get a math tutor instead of taking away allowance. Smart kids require even smarter parents to keep them in line.

❊ **Choose your battles.** Lots of teen behavior can be irritating. But are all your teen's irritating actions worth fighting over and ruining the relationship you've worked so hard to build? As long as your child acts in safe and healthy ways and performs well in school, hang loose and understand that teens like to express themselves. Reinforce the smart decisions he makes and remember this: Your teen exhibits wonderful qualities beyond green-striped hair, belching, and outrageous dress. Strange haircuts grow back, and styles change with the season and peer group. As for belching, this talent eventually loses its power and dies a slow death after you stop reacting to it. Earrings can eventually be put back in the jewelry box. As for tattoos, remind your child that tattoos last for 80 years or are painful to erase, and see if that makes an impression on him before the deed is done. Also keep in mind that messy rooms don't hurt anyone unless items on the floor crawl by themselves, and dishes in the sink and forgotten chores aren't the sum-total of your child's best qualities. Check out www.parentingteens.com and the book *Positive Discipline for Teenagers* by Jane Nelsen for more ideas about raising smart teens.

❊ **Stay connected and supportive.** Let your child know you care about his life. Ask about what's going on. Attend school and outside activities that your child supports. Be truly interested, not fake, about your concern. **Remember:** An unwritten law dictates that your child's activities happen during snow and rain storms and are also timed to coincide with your important work deadlines. But make sure someone represents the family. Horror stories of uncalled rain-soaked games make great family lore. Better than that, your teen remembers that you're willing to go the extra mile to encourage his successes.

❀ **Reinforce that schoolwork comes first.** Let your teen know that activities are great, and friends make life fun, but school remains the number-one job. Emphasize that high school is the time when grades really count toward future plans, whatever they may involve.

❀ **Refrain from lecturing.** Long dissertations usually result in a fight or in your teen spacing out. Lectures lead to nowhere unless the listener wants to hear what's being said. To avoid battles, ask permission to impart your adult wisdom. Then get to the point and be brief. You don't have much time to keep a teen's attention. If your request to give advice is turned down, back off. Your teen has a lifetime to learn. Now doesn't have to be the only occasion. And don't be offended with your teen's attitude that he knows it all anyway. That's a teen thing.

❀ **Shower your teen with unconditional love.** As your child grows older, you may find yourself liking fewer things about him. Similarly, your child may act less approachable and lovable. But even so, send the message loud and clear that no matter what he does, whom he hangs out with, or how much trouble he gets into, he's still your kid, you love him, and you will weather any storms together. *Remember:* Kids who feel secure have higher self-esteem. And higher self-esteem means your teen makes wiser choices in school and when confronted with peer pressure.

❀ **Show you're on your teen's side.** When he makes mistakes, which are inevitable, refrain from "I told you so" or negative comments. Such comments are neither helpful nor necessary. Your teen feels bad enough from natural consequences of his actions. If you respond to your teen as if what he does is awful or dumb, which it may be, he'll look for ways to get into trouble and live up to your interpretations.

How Birth Order Affects Behavior

Certain ages and stages cause kids to act they way they do. But in addition, the birth order of your children can also make a big difference in their behavior. Be aware of your kids' tendencies and be ready to step in when one of them is suffering due to his or her birth order. Table 9-1 lists a few basic birth-order characteristics and explains what you can do to help each of your children.

☺ ☻ ☹ ☺ ☻ ☹ ☺ ☻ ☹ ☺ ☻ ☹ ☹ ☺ ☻ ☹ ☺ ☺ ☻ ☹ ☺

Table 9-1 Birth Order and Resulting Behavior

Birth Order	Personality Tendencies	What You Can Do
First born	Tends to be a leader and a high achiever; however, she also tends to be a perfectionist.	Don't be too demanding. Offer specific praise instead of open-ended praise. If your child builds a great birdhouse, don't say, "That's the best birdhouse I've ever seen." Instead say, "I really like the colors. I bet they'll attract a lot of birds." *Tip:* The single biggest gift parents can give their "perfectionist" child is to *not* model perfectionism.
Second born	Tends to be more easy-going, creative, and playful than his older sibling, which are great traits. However, he also wants to outdo his older sibling if he can, especially if you're constantly praising your first-born child.	Give him as much praise as possible, encourage him to talk about his feelings, stop praising your first-born child in front of him, and show him you love him every way you can.
Middle child	This kid is wedged between an older and younger child, so she tends to be both a leader and a follower, which may cause her to feel left out and insecure. This child may feel compelled to serve as mediator between the other children.	Make her feel special and cherished. One way to do this is to spend one-on-one time with her each day, listening to her, praising her, hugging her, and telling her how much you love her.
Baby of the family	Your youngest is probably creative, outgoing, and affectionate, which is good. However, because the older kids tend to take over and do things for him, he may become dependent on others. The older kids may be a little jealous of your youngest, which can result in bullying.	Stifle any bullying and build confidence and independence in your youngest child by assigning him responsibilities and then praising him for doing a good job.

Chapter 10

Parenting through Tough Times

Parenting is tough, flat out. But at times it's even tougher than usual, like when your kids choose not to follow the rules and boundaries you've established, when your kids suffer the loss of a parent through death or divorce, or when your kids have to move to a new school. This chapter offers advice on how to handle these tough times.

Disciplining and Punishing Your Kids

Discipline is about setting ground rules and boundaries and making your children live by and follow those rules. *Punishment* is what you do when your child chooses not to follow what you've said. The whole point of discipline and punishment is *teaching* your children. It's a learning process.

After you establish your household rules and guidelines, you can't be inconsistent about your decisions. You also can't punish children for something one time and then act like it isn't a big deal the next. Such inconsistency can cause you more trouble than it's worth. In addition, follow-through must be a consequence of your children having broken a rule on purpose. When they break a rule, consider it a test that they're giving you to see whether you're really going to do something. This isn't a test you can afford to fail. (See Chapter 3 for more on setting rules, being consistent, and following through.)

Being in charge without being a tyrant

The fact that you need to discipline your children is not an open invitation to treat them with a lack of respect or decency. Here are some guidelines:

❋ **Let kids be kids.** Allow them to make mistakes, make messes, and get mad and upset. Kids are awkward at times, but they typically aren't malicious or evil. Be careful that you neither punish typical kid behavior nor give them unrealistic expectations that they can never meet.

❋ **Don't make words less meaningful or effective by using them again and again.** If you're always yelling out "No" or "Stop," your words lose their effectiveness after a while. Instead of always saying "No" or "Stop," offer alternatives to whatever your children are start- ing to do. When you see your children starting to color on the walls, for example, say, "Don't color on the walls. Here's a piece of paper. You can color on the paper instead."

When your kids tune you out because you're beginning to sound like a broken record, your entire goal of trying to teach them something goes up in smoke. So try alternative forms of communication for getting your point across. For example, if you're tired of telling your children every day to shut the lid to the toilet, simply put a sign on the wall behind the toilet, like the one shown in Figure 10-1. This gentle reminder keeps you from sounding like you're nagging, and your kids will get the message.

❋ **You don't always have to win.** Discipline shouldn't be a series of wins and losses in an ongoing battle between you and your children. Discipline sometimes can leave room for compromise between you and your kids as long as you get your point across.

Figure 10-1: Sometimes a gentle reminder is all your kids need.

☺ ☹ ☹ ☺ ☺ ☹ ☺ ☺ ☹ ☺ ☺ ☹ ☺ ☺ ☹ ☺ ☺ ☺ ☹ ☺

❀ **Handle situations with gentle guidance.** Being gentle about get-ting your kids to do something is just as easy as yelling and scream-ing at them. Your goal in disciplining is to teach. Your children are more open to listening to and *hearing* you when you express what you want to say in a kind and gentle manner.

❀ **Use enthusiasm to guide your children.** If you're trying to get your children to do something they don't necessarily want to do, approach the situation with great enthusiasm. For example, when you make the process of getting your kids' shoes on them fun and like a game, your children will think doing it is fun.

❀ **Don't harass your children.** You always need to have faith that your kids are going to do what's right. You can't sit waiting for them to do something wrong so that you can pounce on them. Also don't fall into the trap of scolding your kids before anything happens or in anticipation that something may happen.

Using punishment as an educational tool

When you've established your rules and boundaries but your children make the decision not to follow them, it's time for punishment. Punishment is the penalty for breaking rules that you've set up for your children. It's an educational tool you use to show your children why the rules are in place.

The purpose of punishment

Look at punishment as a positive action. Predicting every possible scenario and then handling it in a certain way is impossible, so keep these guide-lines in mind:

❀ **What will the punishment teach your children?** When you fall into the habit of giving the same punishment for the same crime, that punishment may lose its effectiveness and its educational value. If that's the case, then change the punishment. (See the nearby sidebar, "Types of punishment," for options.)

❀ **Your children must always know the reason for the punish-ment.** Make sure your kids fully understand why they're being pun-ished, or the punishment will mean nothing to them.

❀ **Don't establish punishments when you're angry.** Decisions are never good when you make them quickly or in anger. You're also more likely to establish a punishment that's more out of retaliation than with the idea of educating your children in mind.

❀ **Give your children a chance to fix the error.** They need a chance to correct whatever they've done wrong. Resolving the problem is your goal, not punishing whenever possible. For example, if you catch a child in the process of stretching the truth but you can stop her before it turns into a Paul Bunyan–sized lie, you've given your child a chance to correct the error.

❁ **Forgive and forget.** Don't hold grudges against your children. After you've had to punish them, tell them that you still love them and then forget about the crime.

How to handle problems while avoiding punishment

Punishing your kids is not fun, so here are some ways you can handle problems while avoiding punishment:

❁ **Remove the temptation to get into things.** For example, put childproof locks on the cabinets and make sure that the things you don't want your children getting into are out of their reach or inaccessible to them.

❁ **Reconsider what's important.** Did you establish a rule before really thinking it through? Do you really mind when your child throws the furniture cushions on the floor to play with them? Think long and hard before establishing a rule.

❁ **Let your children help you solve problems.** If your daughter can't keep from throwing the skirts she doesn't want to wear on the floor rather than putting them back, ask her to come up with a solution to the problem. Maybe it's time to go through the clothes together and get rid of the ones she can't wear anymore.

❁ **Get in your children's way so they can't get into trouble.** Physically stand in a child's way so that she can't push the plant over in the living room. Tell her she has to leave the plant alone and then get her interested in something else.

❁ **Stay calm and don't yell.** Your kids will most likely tune you out when you yell. Even when a child is yelling at you, don't fall into the trap of yelling back. Gather your patience and keep your voice calm, cool, and relaxed. This strategy not only calms down your child but also shows your child that staying calm is the better way of communicating.

❁ **Explain what you're doing and why.** Knowledge is powerful. If your children understand why you do something or why something isn't allowed, it makes more sense to them. Keep explaining the *why* behind the rules.

❁ **Have your child start over.** When your child talks or behaves rudely to you, ask him to start over. You may even have him leave the room and come back in to approach the situation again. This time, however, ask him to think about what he wants to say and how he should say it.

Types of punishment

Here are some options for punishment:

- **Giving your kids timeouts.**

- **Taking away privileges.**

- **Assigning extra chores.**

- **Punishing by educating.** Say your child is caught stomping on your flower garden. Have her research and write a report about flowers or roots. If she's too young to write, have her draw a picture of flowers and their roots. Look at flowers together and then talk about how roots work. The more your child knows about the consequences of what she's done, the less likely she is to do it again.

If you're wondering why spanking isn't on this list, consider this: Punishment is a learning tool — you're using it to teach your kids something. Does spanking accomplish this? No, not really. Besides, if you hit your child, what does that teach? Whatever you do, your children will imitate, because they look to you for guidance. If you spank your kids, they may be more likely to haul off and smack a sibling or classmate — after all, if it's okay for you to hit, why isn't it okay for them to do the same?

Dealing with the Loss of a Parent through Death or Divorce

Divorce or the death of a parent almost always wounds the heart of a child, even though the child may not show it outwardly. Often, a child shuts down after a divorce, which is a way of protecting herself from the anger, sadness, and confusion she's feeling. The same thing can happen when a parent dies. Unless the child is encouraged to talk about her feelings, the wounds may fester for years and never heal completely.

This section helps you relate to your child's point of view — her hurts, her needs, and the longings of her heart. When you look closely, you can see that your child is going through a difficult time right now, especially if you've become a single parent quite suddenly. So even though you may be having a tough time yourself, your child still needs to be number one in your life as you face your future together. Your child needs you now more than ever before.

Rebuilding physical security

Physical security is feeling that everything is in its place and that all is right with the world. You need to work on rebuilding your child's sense of physical security day after day until she finally feels secure when you tuck her into bed at night.

Likewise, when she walks to school on her own, she may not feel safe because her missing parent always dropped her off on his way to work. So your job is to assure her that you're there for her, to take care of her, to watch out for her, and to make sure nothing bad happens.

 You may need to enlist the help of a neighbor or relative to fill in for you until your child feels more secure. In addition, your child will feel more secure if she knows she can reach you by phone at any time. She also needs to know that the school has your phone number plus the name of a third party (another family member or a friend she knows) who can help out in case of an emergency.

Here are ways you can make your child feel safer:

* **Tell him over and over again how much you love him — never assume that he already knows.**

* **Explain that he will be taken care of and provided for — that he will always have a room and a bed and a place to live.**

* **Tell him he has nothing to worry about — that everything is going to be all right.** With the help of willing grandparents, godparents, aunts, uncles, and other relatives, your child will always have the help he needs — he *will* be all right.

* **Try to stay upbeat, smile, and keep your sense of humor.** This will reassure your child that you aren't always sad and upset. If you're able to laugh, joke, and tease, your child will think everything is okay after all! At the same time, let your child know that it's okay to feel sad or to cry sometimes, too. Tell him that you cry and feel sad yourself, and don't hide your tears from your child — he needs your permission to cry.

Rebuilding emotional security

When a child loses his parent, his emotions are in turmoil. One day he may be lashing out in anger, and the next day he may be curled up in his room, feeling sad and unloved. Both are signs of depression.

☺ ☻ ☹ ☺ ☻ ☹ ☺ ☻ ☹ ☺ ☻ ☹ ☺ ☻ ☹ ☺ ☺ ☻ ☹ ☺

If your child's symptoms don't clear up, you need to take action by seeking out a therapist or counselor who can help him. If you ignore the symptoms, they may get worse, so deal with them the best you can and if you don't see improvement, get some professional help.

Dealing with anger

Your child's anger may show up in various ways: getting into fights at school; complaining loud and long about such things as a teacher or the cafeteria food; or becoming belligerent at home — talking back and acting out. Of course, he's not really angry with his teacher or the cafeteria food. He's angry with you for getting a divorce, he's angry because his life is messed up, and he's angry because he's afraid.

How can you help your child get over his angry feelings? Here are a few suggestions:

- ❈ **Try to have a heart-to-heart talk with your child.** See if you can coax him into verbalizing his feelings. Never interrupt your child when he's talking to you. When he's made his point, it may help for you to repeat what he's said, to be sure you understand what he's trying to get across and to assure him that you're really listening. The key is to assure your child that anger is a normal reaction to what he's been through and that you understand because you feel angry sometimes, too.

- ❈ **Encourage your child to get involved in any type of physical exercise.** Examples are shooting hoops in the driveway, swimming, or something as simple as a brisk nightly walk.

- ❈ **Distract your child with humor.** You can even have a laughing contest. See which one of you can laugh the hardest and the longest.

- ❈ **Encourage your child to write a story about a child whose parents are divorced, including all the hateful feelings the child feels toward his parents.** Explain to your child that he doesn't have to show the story to anyone unless he wants to.

- ❈ **Ask your child to draw pictures of what he's feeling.** This may be a shocking revelation for you, so buckle up for the ride.

- ❈ **Ask a friend, coach, relative, or one of his playmate's parents to talk to him.** See if that person can get your child to open up and talk about how angry he is.

- ❈ **Remember that you are your child's primary role model.** If you can find ways to appreciate each day, find humor in little things, and not be overly reactive, you'll set a good example. If you do blow up, apologize. If your child blows up, try not to take it too personally.

Dealing with grief

Whether your child lost his parent through death or divorce, he grieves the loss. Studies show that healing from the loss of a parent can take up to three years.

When your child's other parent died, especially if it was a sudden death, you may see these tendencies:

- **Your child may ask you questions about death — what it means and what made his parent die.** Explain death in simple terms — that the person can't breathe, move, or think, and that the person's body doesn't work anymore because it is dead. In addition, give the real answer for the death, like "Mommy had a very serious kind of cancer, and she died," instead of using mysterious phrases like "Mommy passed on." Also don't use confusing explanations like "Mommy just went to sleep" because your child will think that sleep is a scary thing that causes someone to die. When your child asks what happens to the person, your answer will depend on your religious or spiritual beliefs.

- **Your child may feel very insecure about being left at daycare or with a babysitter because he's afraid you may never come back.** He may cry and cling to you, not wanting to let go.

- **If you happen to be a little late picking up your child after school, you may see him standing there with his teacher's arm around his shoulders.** When you ask what's wrong, you may discover that your child panicked because you were late.

- **Your child may not show up at the dinner table.** When you look for him, you may find him curled up on his bed sobbing his heart out.

- **When you tuck your child into bed at night, he may panic when you leave the room because he's afraid that, when he wakes up in the morning, you'll be gone, too.**

Here are ways to help him heal:

- **Spend a lot of time with your child, trying to get him to open up and talk about his feelings.**

- **Be patient.** Grief doesn't have a quick fix.

- **Tell him about your own feelings of grief.**

- **Reassure your child that his parent loved him and remind him of the happy times you had together as a family before his parent died.**

☺ ☺ ☹ ☺ ☺ ☹ ☺ ☺ ☹ ☺ ☺ ☹ ☺ ☺ ☹ ☺ ☺ ☺ ☹ ☺

❀ **Encourage your child to talk about his missing parent.**
Speculate together on what Mom might think or say about the day's events. For example, maybe she'd laugh if she knew what you fixed for dinner tonight.

❀ **Establish a steady, dependable daily routine in your lives, with as few interruptions as possible.** Take some time to talk about contingency plans, in case emergencies do pop up.

❀ **Work with your child to create a memory book or photo album about the parent who died.**

❀ **Understand the six stages your child may face as he grieves for his parent: denial, anger, sadness, depression, guilt, and fear.**

Responding to the longing for attention

When a child loses a parent, he becomes a little self-centered, so he resents it when you don't pay as much attention to him as you did before. He also bristles when he's asked to help out more around the house. Your child doesn't understand that you're going through hell and just barely hanging in there yourself. In his mind, everyone has turned against him. He feels deprived, needs more of your time, and longs for time alone with you:

❀ **Your child feels deprived of the other parent's presence, and although he may not say so out loud, he's feeling very lonely.**
Let your child know that you're aware of his lonely, empty feelings. Arrange for him to spend a little extra time with his other parent, if the loss is due to divorce rather than death. If this isn't possible, phone calls, e-mails, or letters may help fill the void.

❀ **Not only does your child miss his absent parent, but he's also feeling the pinch of your schedule.** He needs you to fill the gap created when your spouse died or you got divorced. And this all happens just when you haven't anything left of yourself to give: You're working longer hours just to keep things together financially, and you've taken on many of your spouse's old duties. But you need to try to find more time. Maybe you're involved in more activities than you can handle right now. Practice saying no. In addition, try prioritizing your responsibilities, getting the kids to pitch in at home, structuring errands to save time, getting more organized, accepting help from friends, negotiating with your employer for a more flexible schedule, seeking alternative childcare that requires less driving time, and cutting back on your kids' extracurricular activities for now.

🙂 🙂 ☹ 🙂 🙂 ☹ 🙂 🙂 ☹ 🙂 🙂 ☹ 🙂 🙂 ☹ 🙂 🙂 🙂 ☹ 🙂

❀ **Not only does your child need more attention and affection, but he also wants time with you *alone*.** So how do you carve out private time to spend with each child every day? Try this approach: Make an appointment with each child, even if it's only for ten minutes. (If that's not possible due to chaotic evenings, save the chat until bedtime.) Decide on a quiet private spot for your chat. And while you're meeting, turn off the phone and give instructions to your other kids that you're not to be disturbed unless someone's bleeding.

Getting professional counseling

If you're doing everything you can to help your child recover and get back to her normal self, but you know in your loving, single-parent heart that nothing is working — or that she's developing distressing new habits that seem to persist or become daily behaviors — it may be time for your child to see a professional therapist. Note that it's normal for teens to have fluctuating moods. Persistent mood, behavior, or personality changes are clues that you need to get some outside help.

Here are warning signs that your child may need professional counseling:

❀ He has extreme mood swings (happy one minute and holed-up in his room the next).

❀ She has a short fuse, and everything seems to bother her. She is so irritable that her friends have given up on her.

❀ He was always active and talkative before but has suddenly become inactive and quiet.

❀ She stops associating with her long-time friends and either becomes a loner or starts hanging out with a bad crowd.

❀ He withdraws from normal family fun, such as playing games. If your child won't even go to Pizza Galore with the family, you know you're in big trouble!

❀ She has problems at school, such as cutting class, getting into fights, or plummeting grades.

❀ He seems to be sleeping much more or less than he used to.

❀ She walks and talks in her sleep, or she begins to wet the bed during the night.

❀ He complains frequently about headaches, stomachaches, or feeling tired.

❀ His facial expression is flat, and he has no enthusiasm — even for a good fight with his sister.

* She seems depressed for weeks at a time.

* He takes unnecessary risks and does self-harming gestures, such as scratching his arms with a razor blade. (This is called *self-injury, SI,* or *cutting,* and you can find out more about it at www. self-injury.net.)

* She displays uncharacteristic signs of anger, rebellion, violent behavior, or running away.

 If your teenager shows any signs the he may be considering taking his own life, call the emergency National Suicide Hot Line immediately: 800-SUICIDE (800-784-2433).

Here are danger signs to watch for in your teenager:

* Your teen talks about suicide.

* Your teen starts giving away his possessions.

* Your teen has been deeply depressed for a long period of time, but one day appears to be magically better.

* Your teen seems overly tired most of the time, sleeping during the day on weekends and going to bed early on weeknights.

* Your teen won't tolerate any kind of praise or rewards.

* You teen has become a loner — she won't communicate or take part in family activities.

Moving to a New School

Moving to a new school hurts at any age. But the older your child, the more grumbling you'll hear. That's because older kids leave behind a stronger peer network, their own little society. Therefore, your child may see breaking into a new group as difficult and overwhelming.

Review these survival tips for easing your child's transition into a new learning situation:

* **Prepare your child so that she feels more confident.** Talk about reasons for the move and differences between the old and new school. Discuss your child's feelings throughout the adjustment process. Share how you understand any concerns — maybe ones you've experienced in your day. Stay positive and reassuring about the move and reassure your child that fears will lessen as she gets acclimated.

❋ **Contact the school ahead of time.** Ask to speak to a counselor or someone who can look out for your child. Identify a teacher, counselor, or social worker who can evaluate your child's adjustment and stay in contact with you.

❋ **Request a peer helper to accompany your child to key places, like the lunchroom, for the first few days.** Is anything worse as a child than eating by yourself in a sea of strange faces?

❋ **Visit the school with your child before moving, if possible.** Take a tour. See the classroom, bathroom, and other important locations. Try to meet the teacher or teachers who will educate your child.

❋ **Establish a school routine that includes before- and after-school activities, homework, and bedtime.** Consistent routines build confidence when everything else changes.

❋ **Keep outside activities to a minimum at the beginning.** When your child feels confident about what seems manageable, encourage her to join extracurricular groups, such as choir, band, or sports teams. They provide common interests that may spur school friendships.

❋ **Seek outside professional assistance if your child continues to acclimate poorly.** But give the new situation time and a couple rounds of lower grades on assignments before panicking. If performance *stays* down the tubes, act quickly.

Chapter 11

Family Matters

Family matters can cover a broad spectrum, but some of the more common are handling sibling rivalry, bringing a new baby into the home, blending families after remarrying, and single parenting while maintaining a co-parent strategy with the ex. This chapter provides some guidelines and suggestions you can use every day in dealing with these common family situations.

Dealing with Sibling Rivalry

This section is dedicated to brotherly and sisterly love — and the path you must lead your kids down to get there.

Some guidelines for you, the parent

Here are a few general guidelines for helping you maintain your sanity while molding your children into loving, kind siblings:

* **Don't compare your kids.** Your kids will start resenting each other if you always make them feel that one is better than the other.

* **Don't take sides.** You need to be the neutral party whom everyone can come to. Otherwise, your children may decide they prefer to duke it out rather than come to you.

* **Stay calm.** You need to be the one who can walk in and quietly help everyone else gain control of themselves. If you get upset, too, you won't be much good at helping solve your kids' differences.

* **Keep a sense of humor.** When you help your kids see the humor in situations, the problem is defused.

☺ ☺ ☹ ☺ ☺ ☹ ☺ ☺ ☹ ☺ ☺ ☹ ☺ ☺ ☹ ☺ ☺ ☺ ☹ ☹ ☺

❀ **Set a no name-calling rule.** Name-calling can be hurtful. Whenever someone starts calling someone else names, stop the argument immediately.

❀ **Set a no hitting or pushing rule.** You must consistently teach that hitting or pushing isn't allowed in the family. If children can't touch others in a loving way, they shouldn't touch others at all.

❀ **Give your kids time alone.** If you can sometimes separate your kids and have them play in separate rooms, they won't get on each other's nerves as much and will be more tolerant of each other.

 Arguments typically occur when someone doesn't feel *heard*, so the waters cannot be calmed until everyone feels heard. It isn't vital that everyone agrees, but it is vital that everyone be heard.

Sharing and playing together

The main problem with kids playing together is that, at some point in time, they all spot the same book or stuffed animal — and the fight is on. A variation on that scenario is when one child has a toy and another kid decides that he wants to play with the toy.

What you'll want to do, but shouldn't, is buy duplicate toys for all your kids. If it's something like bicycles, well then, *yes*, it's more fun for each kid to have her own so they can all ride together. Any toy that is more fun if everyone has one (such as Barbies) is great. But if the toy is a game, the answer is no.

 Your kids have to learn to share. They can't go through life thinking that everything they own is theirs and only theirs. You can encourage sharing by showing one child how to offer a toy in exchange for a toy that another child has. Sometimes this works, sometimes it doesn't. The hard part is teaching your children that when someone doesn't want to exchange toys, they'll just have to wait until the toy has been set down. Setting a timer or time limit can sometimes be helpful. Children seem to do better when they understand when their turn starts and ends.

Developing a loving, caring relationship

You must teach your kids to be loving and kind to each other. Make sure that your actions also are a part of the teaching. These actions show your kids how they should behave toward each other:

- **Don't gang up on a child.** You're supposed to be that child's best cheerleader and supporter, not some sporadic antagonist. Ganging up on your children is a surefire way to destroy their trust and any chance of a future relationship with them as adults.

- **Don't tease.** Teasing is sadistic and wrong. Never tease. And be firm with your kids: They are not to tease others.

- **Don't talk badly about a child in front of his siblings.** Again, you need to be your children's best supporter. Your children need to hear that everything you say about them is positive and said in a loving manner.

- **Don't pit your children against each other.** Don't instigate fights or arguments. Your kids are going to have enough confrontations with each other without you adding to their fires.

- **Encourage hugs and kisses between siblings.** When you see your young ones showing affection to each other, let them know how happy you are and encourage them to do so often. This positive reinforcement lets them know that giving affection is a natural and good thing.

- **Teach children how to be gentle.** When you see your toddler belting the baby, take the toddler's hand and gently caress the baby with it. Let your toddler know that's how to touch others. You may also have to show what gentleness is to older children who may not have been around younger children or babies.

- **Teach family togetherness.** Your actions are an important way to teach this. Getting everyone involved in housework, cooking, and playing together is an excellent example of how family togetherness works.

Communicating nicely

Everyone is going to be a teacher to your young children, especially older siblings. Listen closely to how they communicate. If you find that an older child is losing patience and beginning to yell at or be hateful to a younger child, step in and remind the older child that the best way to talk is calmly and nicely. Keep in mind that this behavior probably stems from something else. Find out why he is losing his patience.

Your children look to you as an example. When you remain calm, don't yell, and avoid sarcasm, your kids will pick up this behavior from you. Make sure that you portray a loving, kind, and gentle person. Otherwise, your children may learn from you and their older siblings to

☺ ☹ ☹ ☺ ☹ ☹ ☺ ☹ ☹ ☺ ☹ ☹ ☺ ☹ ☹ ☹ ☺ ☺ ☹ ☹ ☺

❋ **Ignore.** Too many parents ignore their kids when they talk. Make sure that you listen when your children talk to you. Acknowledge what they're saying. And if you hear your children playing and one child is ignoring the other, point it out.

❋ **Be sarcastic.** Like teasing, sarcasm is sadistic. It's being dishonest at the expense of another. Don't do it and don't let your children do it, either.

❋ **Bully.** Children learn to bully from their parents. "You're going to do this because I say so." In other words, "I'm the master, and you're the slave, and that's all the reason I need to give for you to obey me." Alas, everyone usually wants to be the master, which is the core of most arguments and fights between siblings.

Responding to a new baby in the family

Here are some suggestions for handling the arrival of a new baby:

❋ **Don't tell your children that they're getting a new *playmate.*** Newborns don't do much to entertain.

❋ **Don't forget to recognize that your other children are special to you, just like the new baby will be.** Do something special. Give them a gift "from the new baby" or make them a special T-shirt so that they know they're still special in your eyes.

❋ **Don't neglect your older children.** Make an effort to do something with them after the baby comes. Continue to share "dates" with your children.

❋ **Give your children an honest idea of what life will be like when the baby comes.** Tell them that at first the baby will demand a large amount of time and that little brother or sister will mostly just cry, eat, sleep, and not do a whole lot more. Also let them know that Mommy will be tired and will have to take naps to rest.

❋ **Call your local hospital to see whether a sibling class is offered for your children to take.** These classes go over what babies like and dislike, what it's like to change a diaper, and other basic information that your children need to know.

❋ **See whether your local hospital has a sibling class that you can take *with* your children.** These classes give you a general idea of how your children may act with a sibling around and offer some suggestions to prevent them from being jealous.

❋ **Get your kids involved with the preparation for and arrival of the new baby.** Doing so helps your kids feel more like a part of the baby's life. Have them draw pictures to put in the baby's room, pack the diaper bag (after you lay out all the stuff), and fetch diapers or bottles for you.

Being a Successful Stepfamily

The fairytale view of a blended family is that it's like a box of instant brownie mix. Take one marriage, add some kids, throw in a pet and an egg, and in no time at all, you have a wonderful warm family where the kids get along with each other pretty well. In real life, however, a stepfamily faces a lot of problems, especially at first. Here are some of the most common problems and possible solutions.

Bonding with stepchildren

This can be a difficult and frustrating experience for both you and the child. But take heart: Bonds usually develop in time. You can speed up the process by developing your own special connection with each of your stepchildren, which may evolve over time into genuine caring and love for each other. For example, does your stepson enjoy playing golf? Treat him to a round of golf once in a while — just the two of you. You'll be surprised how a common interest can help with the bonding process.

Battling stepsiblings

Don't be surprised if your new family takes a while to blend together. And for many families, a more realistic goal is creating a loving stepfamily where individual needs are honored and accepted. This would be a collection of individuals who can support the family rule and who agree to disagree.

The good news is that kids are adaptable. They'll come around eventually — they just need time to get used to the new family structure. Some family therapists say that kids can take up to three years to adjust. During the adjustment phase, don't constantly force the issue by insisting that one sibling apologize to the other for something he said or did or by forcing the kids to talk about their feelings during a family meeting. And whatever you do, don't expect the oldest child to serve as a free, on-call babysitter. In addition, try your hardest not to play favorites.

Playing the name game

Trying to figure out what stepchildren are going to call their new steppar- ents is a common problem in blended families, especially at first. Don't force the issue. The important thing to remember is that you are not com- peting with or taking the place of the children's other parent. Having them call you by your first name in the beginning may be the simplest. When they're ready, they may dub you with an affectionate mom or dad term, or a name of their own creation, which will be your best reward.

Disliking a new stepchild

Being unable to stand the kid is a real problem because you're going to be living with him or her for many years to come. You need to take a good hard look at your feelings. What is it about the kid that bothers you? Are you sure that junior is the sole source of the conflict? Are you blameless? Can you do anything to ease the negative vibes?

 Not getting along with each other's children is a major reason remarriages fail, so here's a way to lessen the tension when you don't really care for a new stepchild: Look for something good about the kid. Because you fell in love with his mom or dad, look for some traits or qualities that he shares with his parent. Go out of your way to notice the good that he does. Doing so will help you change your attitude toward him, and he'll try harder to please you in the future because he'll see that you value him as a person.

Disagreeing on discipline policies

Disciplining the kids can be a huge problem if you and your spouse don't sit down and decide how you're going to handle it. Most blended families find that the best approach is for the natural parent to discipline the child for at least the first year and for the stepparent to play a supporting role, always following through on the decisions made by the natural parent. Maintaining a united front prevents the kids from playing one parent against the other.

In addition to being supportive of your new partner, you (as the stepparent) can contribute to a mellow family environment by recognizing good behavior from the stepchildren, helping them with their homework, rooting for them at their ballgames, and establishing friendships by being a good listener and sincerely caring about them.

Clashing about the cash

Sit down together (with a financial counselor if necessary) and come up with a budgeting plan. If you both have 10-year-old boys and one receives an allowance of $20 a week while the other gets $5, you have a problem. You need to sort out little discrepancies like this so that each child receives the same amount.

Dealing with all the relatives

At this time in their lives, your kids need all the love they can get. They need to be around grandparents, aunts, and uncles who can help your kids realize that most marriages do hang together for many years. Your ex's relatives and your new partner's parents and extended family members need to serve as anchors in your kids' lives.

Misfiring on all cylinders

If you feel like everyone has his or her own agenda and you're not blending smoothly at all, a family meeting may help. Schedule regular get-togethers where every family member is present and encouraged to talk *without interruption.* Family meetings are a good way to both fix problems and perform routine maintenance. If the kids sense that you're sincere and genuine in your attempts to solve any problems that exist, you may be surprised with their openness and willingness to be part of the solution.

Taking the High Road When Single-Parenting

When you and your spouse get divorced, you're given a choice. You can choose to take the high road or the low road. The high road leads to Victory Mountain. The low road is a slippery path that seems easy at first but offers few rewards and many sorrows.

The high road I'm talking about is also known as successful *co-parenting:* sharing parenting responsibilities with your child's best interests at heart. For the sake of your children, you need to work out an arrangement with your ex-spouse that provides your kids love, stability, and continuity in their lives to help them become well-adjusted, happy adults. That's what this section is about. (You may also want to check out Chapter 10 to learn more about your child's point of view regarding the divorce.)

Note that if you're a single parent due to the death of your spouse rather than divorce, Chapter 10 provides helpful advice and information.

Devising a co-parenting plan with your ex

A *co-parenting plan* is a written agreement between parents who have joint custody of their children. This doesn't mean each parent must share equal time with the children, but they do each have certain responsibilities for care and nurturing.

A co-parenting plan is important because it forces you and the other parent to discuss and agree on responsibilities and joint goals. Joint goals may include such things as providing continuity in the children's lives, agreeing on discipline policies, and saving toward college expenses. Such a plan makes you think about where your kids live, who pays for what, and how much time each parent spends with the children.

Every plan is a little different, especially if it has been custom-designed without the help of an attorney. However, most co-parenting plans should

⚜ Be put together in an unemotional, businesslike, mature manner.

⚜ Be filed with the court or be a private agreement that's binding between parents.

⚜ Include the parents' rules of conduct and communication (see the nearby sidebar, "Conduct and communication rules").

⚜ Contain conditions for the children's medical and dental care.

⚜ Spell out childcare conditions. Include which parent provides and pays for the children's care, or how the expenses and responsibilities are split between the two parents.

⚜ Include a detailed schedule that spells out which parent has custody of which child during the school year, during school vacations, and over holidays or other special family get-togethers.

⚜ Address who provides transportation for the children between the parents' residences.

⚜ Spell out what type of religious training the children receive.

⚜ State educational goals for the children.

⚜ Talk about what happens if one of the parents doesn't follow through on taking the children during designated weekends or vacation days.

⚜ Explain conditions for future catastrophes, such as loss of income, serious illness, or death of one of the parents.

⚜ Explain specific conditions in case one of you moves out of town or out of state in the future.

⚜ Specify the duration of your agreement and what happens if you want to renegotiate its terms in the future.

Getting a tune-up if things are running rough

A co-parenting plan needs regular tune-ups. If your plan is running rough, try this section's suggestions.

Easing transition anxiety

Transition anxiety can be a real problem, especially right after the divorce when all of you are trying to adjust to the co-parenting plan you agreed upon. Here are a few common problems that often pop up during the two-home shuffle and ways to handle them:

☺ ☺ ☹ ☺ ☺ ☹ ☺ ☺ ☹ ☺ ☺ ☹ ☺ ☺ ☹ ☺ ☺ ☺ ☹ ☺

❀ **You and your ex are not very comfortable with each other now that the divorce is final.** Arrange to have pick-ups and drop-offs that don't involve personal contact with each other. For example, drop your children off at daycare in the morning, and your ex can pick them up on the afternoon he takes the kids.

❀ **Your children don't want to go to Daddy's house, and they beg to stay with you.** If your co-parenting agreement has a set schedule for the two-home shuffle, stick by it unless you see serious anxiety setting in. For example, just smile and tell your child, "Daddy would be so disappointed if you didn't come see him — he has so much fun stuff planned for you this weekend. We don't want Daddy to feel sad." Then take your child by the hand and walk him to your ex's car.

❀ **You're feeling bitter.** Don't send your kids off to your ex's home with instructions like "When Daddy gets a phone call, see if it's from his new girlfriend — that Gloria person." Smile and say, "Have fun with Daddy. I love you and I'll see you Sunday night." If this is almost impossible for you to do without breaking your jaw, you may benefit from professional therapy.

Conduct and communication rules

Here are some conduct and communication rules to consider in a co-parenting plan between parents who have joint custody of their children:

❀ Each parent has the right to be involved in the children's lives as situations pop up.

❀ Neither parent bad-mouths the other in front of the kids.

❀ Each parent has the right to see the children's school records, meet with their teachers, and be involved in parent-teacher conferences.

❀ Both parents always let each other know how they can be located if they are out of town or away from home for a long period of time.

❀ Each parent promises to be accessible to the children by telephone, e-mail, regular mail, fax machine, or pager.

❀ Both parents agree to share important information about their children, including problems they may be having, their progress in school, and their achievements in extracurricular activities.

❀ Both parents will be cooperative and accommodating if their child begs to spend more or less time with one of his parents. This is an issue that will need additional, open discussion when it arises.

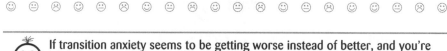

If transition anxiety seems to be getting worse instead of better, and you're seeing warning signs, such as loss of appetite, sleeping problems, long periods of crying, regressive behavior, or any noticeable change in your child's disposition, meet with your ex and talk it over. It may be that your co-parenting plan needs to be revised to accommodate your child's age and emotional stability. Sometimes the solution is something as simple as letting the child spend more time with his preferred parent than before and then easing him into a more balanced schedule as he matures and gets used to the idea of the two-home shuffle. In severe cases, seek advice from a family therapist.

Try to maintain continuity in your kids' lives. Keep major changes to a minimum, maintain two real homes, stay in contact with your children's old friends, encourage open communication between you and your kids and between them and your ex, establish new holiday traditions, and call your child the day before he's scheduled to come to your home. During that phone call, you can tell him about the fun stuff you have in mind while he's with you, and you can go over a list of what he needs to pack in his suitcase for the stay.

Taking that hex off your ex

So getting along with your ex isn't getting any easier, even with this marvelous co-parenting plan you two put together? First of all, you need to realize that every co-parenting situation has rough patches, especially at first. But studies show that things tend to smooth out as the years go by, especially if you *really* try.

Maybe a little forgiveness is in order:

* **Forgive for your kids.** Children whose parents fight all the time tend to feel stressed and have low self-esteem. Research indicates that it matters less the type of family a child grows up in than the amount of conflict (parental tension) the child must endure.

* **Forgive for you.** Any person filled with poisonous attitudes may catch every bug that comes along, have aches and pains he never had before, feel tired and run down, and even become seriously ill. A bitter person can also become emotionally ill, which means that he may suffer depression, feelings of poor self-worth, and other psychological pain.

* **Forgive for your co-parenting plan.** How on earth are you ever going to make it work if you're continually bickering with your ex over every little thing?

Maybe, also, you need to examine a few innovative ways to negotiate with your ex. If what you've been doing isn't working, and you're at each

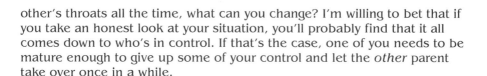
other's throats all the time, what can you change? I'm willing to bet that if you take an honest look at your situation, you'll probably find that it all comes down to who's in control. If that's the case, one of you needs to be mature enough to give up some of your control and let the *other* parent take over once in a while.

Avoiding the biggest mistakes made by single parents

Single-parenting is an incredibly difficult job. As a matter of fact, parenting is difficult for two parents in a traditional family unit, so trying to go it alone is even more difficult. In the process of trying to be the best parent you can be, it's easy to fall into one of these single-parent traps:

* **Heaping more onto your kids' plates.** If you're like many single parents, you want your child to achieve and excel. It's only natural for you to want the best for your child, but overloading her with activities is a mistake. If your child has one or two extracurricular activities at a time, that's plenty. Your kid needs downtime, time to relax and be silly, and time to do absolutely nothing!

* **Encouraging your kids to be private detectives.** Don't pump your children for information about your ex, your ex's lifestyle, or your ex's squeeze, and don't ever suggest that they watch for stuff when visiting their other parent (like "See if you can find out where she's going after work").

* **Denying yourself a social life.** If you're like so many single parents, you're afraid that dating or having a social life of your own may hurt your kids, especially if they've been through a painful divorce. You tend to carry guilt around with you, and if you do date, it's on the sly so your kids don't find out about it.

* **Allowing your kids' traits to ring your bell.** It's quite common for you to be disturbed when you recognize your ex's traits in your kids. If your ex really irritates you, it's possible you dislike things about her that are actually positive traits! So don't take it out on the kids — it's not their fault that your ex drives you nuts.

* **Expecting your children to deliver messages to your ex.** Sending a message with your kids is easier than calling your ex yourself or delivering the message in person, but it's not fair to your kids.

* **Getting sucked into power plays.** A *power play* is a verbal struggle that develops when your child tries to bully you into backing down on something you've asked him to do or on a rule that you've established. His voice becomes louder and louder as you respond in kind. When you're sucked into one of these power plays, no one wins. Enforcing a rule calmly is much better, because it protects

your child's sense of dignity. To avoid these power plays, don't give in to your child's antics.

❀ **Being a poor role model.** You, as a single parent, are a role model for your kids, whether you like it or not. Watch for any bad habits (smoking, getting drunk, swearing, fighting with your ex, and so on) that can poison your kids, and strive to be the best role model you can possibly be.

❀ **Allowing your kids to con you.** Your children know how to work you, and when they want something, they play on your guilt. Whether they're crying out for designer jeans or a McDonald's Happy Meal, you're the one who decides whether you want to buy it or can afford to spend the money. So be strong.

❀ **Failing to establish boundaries.** Don't be a wishy-washy parent who isn't consistent with what's okay and what's not. If talking back is unacceptable, then it must always be unacceptable. If your child throws his toys across the room every time he doesn't get his way, don't ignore him part of the time and punish him other times.

❀ **Pushing your ex's buttons.** Doing so comes from maintaining your anger toward your ex-spouse. If you maintain this pattern and keep the tension high between you and your ex, it will likely damage your child. If you're having trouble controlling the anger you feel toward your ex, consider joining a single-parent support group or seeking the help of a professional therapist.

❀ **Refusing to consider professional therapy.** You may be experiencing an incredible amount of stress as you strive to cope as a single parent, and sometimes a single parent needs a time-out from the kids. Parental stress hot lines allow a frantic parent to reach a well-trained volunteer who can be a calming influence or offer helpful suggestions. Crisis centers have also been established to assist single parents who realize they're near the breaking point and are unable to cope with the children. Check the Yellow Pages to find help in your community. To start your search, look under headings similar to these: Crisis Intervention Service, Mental Health Services, or Social Service Organizations. In addition, many other professionals are there to help you, including family therapists, psychologists, and counselors available through your church or single-parent support groups.

Chapter **12**

It Takes a Village: Sharing in Parenting

Being a parent is difficult. Moms especially seem to have it in their minds that they're supposed to be Supermom — able to handle it all with ease, with a smile on their faces and a clean house, and, worse yet, looking good while doing it. More and more dads are put in this position, too. But hey, guys — you can't do it all. It takes a village.

Co-Parenting: Being Part of a Team

Parenting is teamwork. It's about planning ahead so that you and your partner can act as full-time parents together, working toward a family environment. In turn, having a strong family environment gives kids a strong foundation for finding out who they are, thus making them secure individuals. The trick is making this parenting team work together when both parents have different backgrounds, experiences, and expectations about parenting.

Note that if you're a single parent, this section is still for you. Your co-parent can be a roommate, a grandparent, an uncle or aunt — anyone in your life who can be there to help you raise your kids. (In addition, you may want to check out the section "Finding Opposite-Sex Role Models if You're a Single Parent," later in this chapter, for specific help in that particular area.)

The business of having fun together

Many statements about parenting are contradictory and even quite the opposite of the truth. A line from the movie *Honey, I Blew Up The Kids* is one example that goes "Daddies are for fun; mommies mean business." But do you know what happens when daddies never partake in the really

tough stuff? Mommies become resentful. And daddies — I hope you know by now — that is never a good thing. You both must be involved in every aspect of raising your kids. Mommies and daddies are for fun. Mommies and daddies can mean business.

Why is having fun a business? Because unless you schedule your activities, work and play alike, nothing happens. Putting the kids to bed can be a great time that can turn into wonderful memories — that is, if you do it together. It also takes less time when you work together to complete family chores so that you can schedule fun time together, as a family *and* as a couple.

Sharing housework

Sharing housework is a sore subject with many families. One partner usually feels like he or she is doing *all* the work, or another may always complain about the house not being tidy.

The housework issue doesn't necessarily mean that you have to divide up the chores equally so that everyone has five each. It means that you divide the chores up equitably, which means fairly or reasonably.

Sit down and make a list of things that you're both willing and able to do. If you hate vacuuming, let your partner do it. If your partner detests the laundry, you do it. If you both hate doing the dishes, then do them together and get that chore out of the way. (***Remember:*** The time will come when your children can do the dishes for you.) And if you become bored with your regular chores, keep things interesting by making changes to your chore schedule every week or so.

 Come up with an agreeable plan as to what a "clean house" means to both of you. What is the standard that you're both willing to live with? Keep in mind that, with kids, having a clean house all the time may be a pipe dream that may not ever happen. So pick your battles.

Handling mutual decision-making

As co-parents, you and your partner are likely to disagree about how to handle certain situations with your child. You must treat those situations delicately. You don't want to turn a coloring-on-the-walls incident into a raging debate about who's going to sleep on the couch, especially when your little one is standing there absorbing everything you're saying.

Here are some suggestions for handling mutual decision-making:

* **Don't argue about discipline — especially in front of your kids.**
  They interpret this as one parent taking their side while the other

doesn't. They store this information away and eventually use it against you — not in an evil kind of way, but they remember it and bring it up later. **Remember:** Keep arguments or disagreements about your children private. Even though it's okay for them to know that you have disagreements, they don't need to hear the back-and-forth arguments that their parents have about them. Whenever you find yourself heading into a child-based argument, call for a timeout, which means that you pick a time to start the conversation again when you can be alone with your partner.

❀ **Respect each other's parenting ideas.** Child-raising ideas come from your background. They're based on how you were disciplined and your life experiences. Your partner has a background, too, complete with his or her ideas and expectations, so be open to what your partner has to suggest. Don't always assume that your way is the right way.

❀ **Agree on the decision.** If both parents agree on a solution to a problem or a rule to enforce, then the solution will be enforced. If one parent disagrees, that parent won't enforce the rule. It's that simple. So when confronted with a situation that requires a solution, both parents must agree on that solution. If you can't agree, then come up with another solution.

❀ **Talk out disagreements.** You both need to feel comfortable with the outcome and agree to household rules and how to handle incidents in which those rules are broken. When you're inconsistent with the rules, your child will likely become confused, probably decide not to listen to either one of you, or — worse yet — play you both off of each other.

❀ **Never jump into ongoing situations.** If you walk into a room where your partner already is handling a situation, try to keep quiet. Things aren't always as they appear, and you probably don't know exactly what's going on.

❀ **Don't gang up on your child.** If you both see something happening that shouldn't, let one parent deal with it. Neither of you wants to appear as though you're ganging up on your child. If you see that your partner is having trouble, offer to step in and help.

Sharing childcare

When you're busy with the kids, it may seem there's little that your partner can do to help. Wrong! To be a ton of help, your partner can

❀ **Pick up the clutter.** It's always baffling that whole families can walk over a napkin on the floor, as if someone placed it there as a sacrificial piece of garbage and only certain holy hands are allowed to touch it. Instead, pick up the napkin, as well as toys, blankets, bottles, or towels that you see lying around.

- ✹ **Share the childcare duties.** Take turns changing diapers, putting the kids to bed, giving baths, feeding, helping with homework — and whatever else needs to be done to take care of your kids.

- ✹ **Give your partner some free time alone every now and then.** As much as you love your children, sometimes getting away for an hour or so to spend time alone is good. This goes for both parents.

Part of caring for your child is sharing the ties that bind. In other words, you'll want to spend bonding time with your child. Make dates where just Mom and child or Dad and child can go out and do things together. This is a great time to grow closer to your child and spend uninterrupted time talking to your child. These outings don't always have to be costly. Go out and run errands, go grocery shopping, or just go for a walk or a bicycle ride.

Finding Opposite-Sex Role Models If You're a Single Parent

A *role model* is someone who offers a positive example of a particular type of behavior or social role that you'd like your children to emulate. In other words, you want your kids to hang out with adults they can look up to and who provide inspiration and guidance for their lives. You, as the parent, are a major role model for your kids, but if you're a single mom or dad, you may want to find opposite-sex role models for your sons and daughters, too.

Why kids need a female role model

Your children need to be around feminine role models, especially if they have little or no contact with their mother:

- ✹ **Your daughter:** She especially needs this influence because she won't know what's expected of her as a wife and mother unless she observes women in these roles. Strive to find strong, successful women. Of course, just because a woman is strong and successful doesn't mean she's a perfect person; the more role models you provide, the easier it will be for her to compare and be impressed with those who do have stellar qualities. You can also take your daughter to see movies that are based on real-life stories of admirable women and provide her with autobiographies of women who have achieved greatness, such as Amelia Earhart and Eleanor Roosevelt.

- ✹ **Your son:** He needs the influence of positive female role models not only because it exposes him to women, who express their emotions more easily than many men, but also because it teaches your

☺ ☹ ☹ ☺ ☺ ☹ ☺ ☺ ☹ ☺ ☺ ☹ ☺ ☺ ☹ ☺ ☺ ☺ ☹ ☺

son what to expect from a wife and mother. A positive female role model can bolster his self-esteem in small ways, such as by complimenting him on his new hairstyle or clothing. Depending on the circumstances, a boy being raised by a single father may also feel that his mother didn't want him, and in this kind of circumstance, a positive female role model can be invaluable to his self-esteem.

Why kids need a male role model

Your children don't have to have Daddy around as a role model, but they sure need some type of male influence:

🌼 **Your son:** He needs a positive male role model because research shows that if he doesn't have one, he tends to act out his anger and be more physically aggressive and difficult with friends and teachers. By watching a mature older male, he finds out what's expected of him when he finds himself in one of the roles of husband and father.

🌼 **Your daughter:** She needs a positive male influence in her life, especially when she starts to date boys. A girl growing up in a singlemother household, with little or no contact with her dad, may have the mistaken idea that her father deserted her because she's unattractive or undesirable. She needs the influence of a strong male figure who makes her feel good about herself. Providing a male role model who challenges her to be the best she can be is also a good idea.

How to find role models for your kids

Here are a few ways to provide role models for your kids:

🌼 **Join single-parent organizations.** Get involved in a single-parent organization that has regular social activities involving single moms, dads, and their kids. Parents Without Partners, for example, has just about equal numbers of single mothers and fathers, so the organization's get-togethers provide a way for your kids to soak up the positive influence provided by the single dads and single moms.

🌼 **Contact Big Brothers/Big Sisters International.** Get in touch with your local Big Brothers/Big Sisters organization for a role model to mentor your child on a regular basis. Many teachers also get involved pairing up a student with a Big Brother or Big Sister, so chat with your child's teacher.

🌼 **Request certain coaches and teachers.** Always request opposite-sex coaches and teachers for your kids, if they're available.

☺ ☺ ☹ ☺ ☺ ☹ ☺ ☺ ☹ ☺ ☺ ☹ ☺ ☺ ☹ ☺ ☺ ☺ ☹ ☺

✺ **Hang out with two-parent families in your circle of friends.**
When friends invite you and your kids to join them for a trip to
Disneyland, a day water-skiing on the lake, or a weekend hiking and
camping trip, say yes. Sometimes a single parent feels like the lone
duck on one of these outings with two-parent families, but get over
it! Your kids need the influence.

✺ **Encourage sleepovers at friends' homes.** If your son or daughter
is invited to spend the night at the two-parent home of a friend, do
everything you can to see that it happens. Even a simple sleepover
once in a while gives your kids a chance to be around a male or
female role model. *Remember:* Check things out ahead of time so
that you feel assured that your child is in a safe environment when
spending time with role models — especially when sleeping over at
friends' homes.

✺ **Entertain at home.** Ask a few single moms and dads and their kids
over for a potluck dinner, a movie night, or a just-for-the-fun-of-it
party. That way, your kids have a chance to interact with single dads
or moms.

✺ **Find a surrogate.** Find a friend who is willing to serve as a surrogate Daddy or Mommy, someone your child can confide in when he
or she doesn't want to talk to Mom or Dad.

✺ **Look into loving relatives.** Your family is probably full of uncles,
aunts, grandpas, grandmas, and older cousins who may be honored
to fill in occasionally as role models. You may have to toss a few
subtle suggestions out from time to time, such as "Michael would
sure love to go to a hockey game with you and Jim once in a while"
or "Would you like to come watch Trisha play in the state basketball
playoffs next week?" Grandma and Grandpa can be a great help with
your children, especially during difficult times. If you're a single
mother, your kids need the positive role modeling of Grandpa in
their lives, and if you're a single father, they need the influence of
Grandma.

Finding Good Childcare

Picking a childcare provider is scary, plain and simple. Giving your child to
someone and hoping that the provider will love and care for your child the
way you do is difficult. This section examines some childcare options and
is meant to help you make good decisions about who will watch your child.

Whatever you choose as a means of childcare, always consider the location.
As is true with real estate, everything is *Location! Location! Location!* You
want something that's close to home and, preferably, close to work — or at
least close to whoever will be picking up your child.

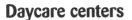

Daycare centers

Daycare centers are easy to find, they're staffed with teachers, and your child's day is usually organized with arts, crafts, and music. Look for a daycare that actually tries to teach the basics, like the alphabet, counting, and printing.

The good part about daycare centers is that you can find one where teachers have teaching credits or credentials, and the environment is bright and clean. Your child will have other kids to play with and a nice area to play in. Furthermore, these centers are required to have licenses and are reviewed by the licensing agencies to make sure they're following daycare standards.

 If you find a daycare center that doesn't have a license, turn around and run. Places that aren't licensed are not held accountable by anyone to operate safe and sanitary centers.

The bad part about daycare centers is that some parents — who feel too obligated to work in order to think sensibly — often send their sick children to daycare instead of keeping them at home. That means if you put your children in a daycare center, they will get sick, harboring the latest strain of flu from their playmates. You also may have problems finding a daycare center that accepts children who haven't yet been potty-trained. Or the center may just charge you an extra fee to change diapers.

A third concern with daycare centers is that your children may not get much individualized attention, especially when classes are at full capacity. What is full capacity? It depends on the ages of the children and the square footage available at the center. Call your local Child Welfare Department to find out what your local requirements are.

 Corporate daycare centers, supported by individual companies, are becoming more popular. These centers are in the same location as the company, so your child simply goes to work with you every day. If a daycare center is the route you're going to take, check to see whether your company has a corporate daycare center available. Your child can go to work with you, you can visit your little one during the day, and you can even have lunch together.

Private sitters

The old-fashioned babysitter is still alive, and two options are available: at his or her home or at your home.

Generally, you have to be careful with private sitters. Most aren't governed by any regulations unless they're watching more than a certain number of kids, and that number varies from state to state. No certification means they don't have to comply with any cleanliness, health, or safety standards.

> You don't want to leave your kids with a sitter of any kind without giving the sitter permission to authorize medical treatment in case of an accident. Make photocopies of the slip shown here; then fill it out and leave it with your sitter when you leave him or her alone with your children.

_____ has my permission to authorize medical
Fill in the complete name of your sitter

treatment to my child(ren), _____,
in case of a medical emergency.

Signed,

_____
Sign your complete name

Sitters who care for kids at their house

The good news about private home sitters is that they're usually less expensive than daycare centers or sitters who come to your home. They typically have a small group of children, so your child gets more attention than at daycare, and if your child is ill, you can usually still use the sitter (although some sitters won't allow sick children). Some home sitters will allow your schedule to be a little more flexible, as opposed to daycare centers, which require you to pick up your child at a certain time or else pay a humongous fine.

The bad news is that private home sitters may not have a backup person for when they become sick. They also may not be required to be licensed (it varies from state to state), so there's no way to monitor their work. You also have to be careful that your private home sitter doesn't decide to take every December off to take hula lessons in Hawaii. Having a sitter gone for an entire month can really leave you in a lurch.

When interviewing a private sitter who works out of his or her home, go to the prospective sitter's house to see whether it's clean and tidy. Are there safety locks on cabinets and on electrical plugs? Is there a place for kids to play?

In addition to asking the questions listed in the "Questions to ask when childcare hunting" section of this chapter, also ask about the number of kids the private sitter takes care of at one time. Does the sitter ever leave the house with the kids? Does the sitter entertain much company during the day? Is the sitter certified in CPR and first aid?

You may also be concerned if the private sitter doesn't plan and schedule activities for the day. You want someone whose main concern is taking care of your child. Finding a sitter who offers arts, crafts, and games similar to those used at daycare centers would be nice, because you don't want someone who looks at childcare as going about the day as usual only with someone else's kid hanging around.

Sitters who care for your kids at your house

When you have a private sitter who comes to your home, you can determine what you want your children to do all day. If you want them involved in art projects or park outings, you're the one who makes the decisions. You also don't have to worry about other children making your child sick or you having to stay home from work with a sick child. If you're really lucky, your sitter may also do some housework.

The only problem with private sitters is that they're hard to find, they tend to be expensive, and you need a backup person for when they get sick. You also aren't able to see how the sitter does during the day, because no one is around except the sitter and your kids; this person coming into your home every day will be alone with your children. Similarly, a sitter isn't required to be licensed.

Finding someone you already know and trust is great. If that isn't an option, then remember to thoroughly check references, and if the sitter is willing, have him or her fingerprinted by your local law enforcement agency. And remember that most of the questions in the "Questions to ask when childcare hunting" section of this chapter also apply to private sitters, so be sure to ask before you hire anyone.

Co-op programs

A co-op program is organized by a group of parents who all share baby-sitting time. If you have a full-time 9-to-5 job, this program won't work. But if you work part-time or don't work outside your home, a co-op program is a great way to get a baby-sitter for lunch dates or just time away to do shopping. Payment is made in kind. In other words, you baby-sit for other members of your group when they need a sitter. Hours are logged so that one parent isn't doing all the sitting, and another is doing all the shopping. It works out so that everyone gets equal time. When you first meet with your co-op group, be sure to go over all the rules, especially situations regarding sick children.

After-school programs

Many daycare centers, private sitters, and even some public schools offer after-school programs. These programs are for school-age children who need someplace to go after school until their parents can pick them up.

You need to ask the same questions about after-school programs that you do when your children need an all-day caregiver. In addition to these questions, you need to find out the following:

* Is the afternoon organized?

* Is time scheduled for kids to do their homework?

* Do kids get an afternoon snack, or are they expected to bring their own?

* What arrangements are in place for transporting children from their school to the after-school program (when it's at a different location)?

* How are kids released to their parents?

Questions to ask when childcare hunting

You must be aggressive when hunting for childcare. Don't be shy or timid; don't hesitate to ask questions and poke your nose around where it probably doesn't belong. Be bold and brave. You're making an important decision, and you have every right to act like an overprotective parent — maybe even on the paranoid side.

Arm yourself beforehand with questions. Write them down and document the answers. When you've researched all the places and people who are possible candidates, sit down and go over the answers. With a written record, you won't have to try to remember which person said what and who promised this or that. Use the questionnaire in Table 12-1 to make your search easier.

Table 12-1 Questions to Ask a Potential Babysitter

Question	Answer
May I have some names and phone numbers of parents who currently have their children attending here or of parents whose children you have cared for in the past?	❑ Yes ❑ No
Do you allow visitation during the day?	❑ Yes ❑ No
What kind of snack or lunch program do you offer?	

☺ ☺ ☹ ☺ ☺ ☹ ☺ ☺ ☹ ☺ ☺ ☹ ☺ ☺ ☹ ☺ ☺ ☺

Question	Answer
May I see the play areas?	❏ Yes ❏ No Note _____ _____ _____
What is the procedure for releasing the children at the end of the day?	_____ _____ _____
What are the rules regarding sick children?	_____ _____ _____
Do you give out medications? If so, what is your policy?	❏ Yes ❏ No _____ _____ _____
What will you do if my child gets injured?	_____ _____ _____
If your caregiver calls you and/or a doctor only for an emergency, what constitutes as an emergency?	_____ _____ _____
What are your fees?	_____ _____ _____
Do you have a late pick-up charge?	❏ Yes ❏ No _____ _____ _____
What kind of payment schedule do you have?	_____ _____ _____
Do you allow uncharged time for vacations?	❏ Yes ❏ No _____ _____ _____
What is your teacher-to-child ratio?	_____ _____ _____

continued

Table 12-1 Questions to Ask a Potential Babysitter *(continued)*

Question	Answer
What are your teacher qualifications?	
What is the turnover rate of your teachers?	
Do you do background checks on your employees?	❏ Yes ❏ No
How do you discipline children?	
What kind of communication will I have with my child's caregiver?	
How well does my child have to be potty-trained?	
What is your daily curriculum for the children here?	
Do you have a naptime during the day?	❏ Yes ❏ No
What is your policy on children who no longer take naps?	
Can I see your last licensing report?	❏ Yes ❏ No
Do you have NAEYC (National Association for the Education of Young Children) accreditation?	❏ Yes ❏ No

Chapter 13

No Slurpy Soup, Please: Instilling Good Social Skills

Although teaching good manners to your children isn't difficult to do, the greatest challenge is setting a good example and pointing out the reasons for your behavior. The less you talk and the more you demonstrate, the more effective you are.

Long before you think about teaching your kids some of the basics of good manners, they shape their own actions by watching and listening to you. Parents are full-time role models for their children, and — without putting too much pressure on parents — the entire world depends on them to turn out civilized, polite members of the next generation. This chapter helps you do just that.

Teaching Basic Good Manners

Good manners begin at home and should be taught by parents. Here are some guidelines that you can use:

❀ **Teach your kids to be kind to others.** Stress the importance of treating others the same way they'd like to be treated, especially when you see your children doing something that you know they themselves don't like.

❀ **Help your children understand their actions.** Help them understand the harm they can cause by doing or saying thoughtless and unkind things.

❀ **Show them the way.** Children do whatever they have to do to express themselves. Sometimes that comes off looking and sounding pretty bad. Playing a role reversal game with your children can help show them how to handle situations.

❁ **Be a good role model.** When you want your children to show good manners and respect, you must also practice good manners and respect. Say *please* and *thank you* to your children as well as other people, admit your mistakes, apologize, and treat people, in general, with kindness and respect.

❁ **Share.** Share with your children so they understand the importance of sharing with others. Compliment them when you see them sharing with others.

❁ **Keep them healthy.** Children, like adults, have more difficulty following rules and using their manners when they're tired or hungry. Kids need sleep and nutritious foods not only to survive but also to flourish and maximize their potential.

❁ **Practice family politeness.** Everyone in the family must follow a "use your manners" policy in which, for example, no request is considered unless the person asking says "please" or "thank you." This goes for you, too!

❁ **Teach them to write thank-you notes.** Teach your children the importance of thanking people for gifts or nice deeds. Show them how to write notes or help them draw pictures. Make sure the letters are sent promptly.

❁ **Praise good behavior.** Praise is a wonderful teacher and reinforcement. Tell your children how proud you are when you notice them being polite and following the "please" and "thank-you" guidelines that you've set.

Maintaining Household Harmony by Setting Etiquette Expectations

The easiest way to maintain peace in your home is to make it clear to everyone what you expect from each person in various situations. If you prepare children (and adults, too) for what they will encounter and explain to them what type of behavior is appropriate, you're bound to have fewer problems and squabbles.

Setting a good example at the table

Children learn table manners, like most behaviors, from parental example. Although a very young child may be incapable of manipulating a knife and fork, when the time comes to pick up a piece of silverware, that same youngster will know what to do because he has watched you do it for months. If you conduct yourself sensibly, your children will, too, as soon as they're able.

This brings you to the rock-bottom foundation of etiquette. You know every one of these little "rules," but do you *always* follow them? Here's a list of just a few ways to set a good example for your youngsters:

* Come to the table on time, clean, and suitably dressed.
* Wait for everyone to be seated before starting the meal.
* If it is your custom to offer a blessing, do so as if you mean it.
* Ask for items to be passed instead of reaching for them.
* Take fair portions, considering the number of others at the table.
* Use a knife rather than the side of a fork to cut food.
* Take manageable bites.
* Don't speak with food in your mouth.
* Don't make a fuss over items you don't like.
* Wait until everyone has finished before leaving the table.
* Avoid confrontations and conflicts while dining.
* Express gratitude and satisfaction to the preparer of the meal.
* Deal with spills and accidents calmly.
* Follow the family rules that you invent — and be consistent.

Dining out as a family

Preparations for eating in a restaurant should begin at home. Children may have a tough time in restaurants. The food is unfamiliar, and the surroundings are not at all as they are accustomed to at home and may be noisy and overstimulating for a child. The seating may be uncomfortable, and your impatient kids are forced to wait for a server to bring things. Perhaps most challenging is visualizing the actual item from a menu description or an interpretation by an adult. Youngsters are often disappointed with the food they receive, not because it isn't well prepared but because they were expecting something else.

 If you understand the difficulties of being a kid in a restaurant, you're better equipped to ease your children into the world of dining out.

In your role as a teacher, try to help your kids understand these basics of good restaurant behavior:

* Wait patiently to be seated.
* Wash hands before beginning the meal.

❀ Speak softly.

❀ Remain seated at the table (except for an escorted bathroom visit if necessary).

❀ Quietly play with toys or crayons while waiting for food to arrive or others to finish.

The best way to introduce children to the restaurant experience is to take them to a child-friendly establishment (restaurants with children's menus typically fall into this category) at a time of the day when it isn't crowded. A cafeteria is a good place to start. When youngsters can see the actual food items before making a commitment, they make better choices. A little guidance can keep them from concentrating on desserts.

To prevent temper tantrums in restaurants, talk to your children before leaving the house to let them know what to expect and what you expect from them. Setting their expectations beforehand helps you avoid upset and the need to discipline at the restaurant. Explain to them what type of food is on the menu before you leave, and discuss possible choices or whether they may have dessert.

Arrive at the restaurant prepared by bringing a quiet toy or crayons to keep your children occupied. Don't expect the restaurant to provide these things to entertain your children.

The waitstaff is there to provide you with food service, not janitorial service. If your little darlings choose to put more food on the table and floor than in their mouths, try to clean up as best you can before leaving.

Plan ahead so your child succeeds. Many children under the age of 5 cannot sit in a chair quietly for more than 30 to 45 minutes. If you know your child's time limit, you can plan accordingly by going to restaurants where you can make reservations or at a time when the wait is minimal. If you use your allotted time waiting for a table, then the actual eating experience won't be fun for you *or* your child.

A restaurant is not a playground for children. They should learn early that they are to remain at the table. Never leave them unsupervised or allow them to run wild around the restaurant – not even at child-friendly establishments. Young children don't understand the difference between dining in a fine restaurant and dining in a fast-food restaurant. If they're allowed to misbehave in one, why not in the other?

If your children are obviously disturbing other diners in the restaurant, take them out of the room until they calm down.

Using courtesy regarding the telephone

A gray area exists between child psychology and etiquette for children. Telephone usage falls into this uncertain area. On the one hand, you want your children to learn how to communicate effectively, but on the other hand, you don't want them to take over the phone as their own personal property. There comes a time in every toddler's life when he or she falls in love with the telephone and looks forward to every opportunity to use it. A bit later on, when your child becomes a teenager, the love affair may become an obsession — and that can cause major headaches for you, the parent.

Safety is also involved. Every child who is old enough to manage it should know how to dial 911 and stay on the line. Don't overlook your responsibility to teach your children how to dial 911 as well as when to use it (for emergencies only — and be sure to explain what an emergency is and what it isn't).

Here are some suggestions regarding children, phone etiquette, and phone safety:

- **Do not inflict toddlers on others via the phone.** When Grandma calls, don't put your 2-year-old on the line. You may think that it's cute, but Granny may not be thrilled to get an earful of silence when checking in from London.

- **Discuss with other parents your desires regarding child-to-child calling times.** Establish the best time of day and a maximum duration for calls between kids, and then enforce the rules.

- **Teach children to answer the phone by saying, "Good afternoon, Miller residence."** (Have them substitute your last name, of course.) Also teach them not to get into conversations with strangers.

- **Teach children how to take a message.** If a child is old enough to answer the phone, the child is old enough to take a name and number and promise a callback.

- **Make sure that teenagers participate in equal access to telephones in the same way that they participate in equal dessert at dinnertime.** Establishing a time limit for each call and a between-call time interval is fair. Otherwise, you won't receive incoming calls for anyone else in the house.

- **Don't worry if your Sarah dials up her friend John to arrange a meeting at the mall.** The old business about girls not calling boys has pretty much disappeared.

- **Examine your monthly telephone bills carefully.** You may discover that one of your children is using the phone in a way that displeases you. Kids tell each other about little scams and pranks that they can play with the phone. Discuss exceptional charges and notations with the child. The telephone company has elaborate means by which it can detect these types of infractions, and it will contact the subscriber with full details. If you learn of your child's telephone misconduct from the phone company, be prepared to take stern measures to prevent such behavior in the future.

✱ **If your children have their own line, consider placing limits on it.** Your telephone company can provide useful limits on a telephone line to keep your children — and your phone bills — safe. For example, you can arrange to block all outgoing 900-number calls and all long-distance calls. In other words, the youngster can use the telephone only for local calls.

Here are a few additional things to keep in mind:

✱ Although identifying yourself to the answering party is considered polite, teenagers are especially sensitive about having their calls screened. So if your teen's friends don't identify themselves, try to avoid the temptation to ask who's calling unless you absolutely need to know.

✱ Kids tend to speak loudly and rudely when they want to use a phone that another person is currently using. Be sure to require patience of them — if being loud works, they'll try it the next time.

✱ Teach your children at an early age that when Mommy and Daddy are speaking to someone on the phone, they are not to be disturbed (except for an emergency). Don't reward your kids when they tug on you or whine to get your attention.

✱ When you pick up the phone and the call is for another person in the household, walk over to that person and give the message. Don't shout "Nathan! Phone!" at the top of your lungs. Require the same politeness from your kids.

Divvying up the household chores

Sharing the household chores is important in learning responsibility and respect for others and for a household. Each week or month, trade specific duties so that one child is not always responsible for the same chore. Doing so prevents boredom and teaches children the various jobs around the house.

The first rule of any well-mannered household should be to clean up after yourself. That goes for dishes, countertops, spills, toys, and dirty clothing. The cardinal rule in a household should be to leave things the way they were found. By teaching your children early that you expect this behavior of them, you'll have a happier life as a parent of teenagers.

A corollary to leaving things as you found them is that, if it's empty, you throw it away or recycle it. Don't allow your children to put an empty milk

☺ ☺ ☹ ☺ ☺ ☹ ☺ ☺ ☹ ☺ ☺ ☹ ☺ ☺ ☹ ☺ ☺ ☹ ☹ ☹

carton back in the refrigerator with just a drop left, or a bag of chips back in the cupboard with just the crumbs! In the same vein, tell children that they're responsible for being good inventory clerks. If they eat or drink the last of something, they should tell the person who does the shopping. Parents can make this task easier by posting a list for needed items on the refrigerator with a pen or pencil handy — make it easy for your kids to help you out, and they will.

Using fair share as an expression of courtesy

For everyone in a household, the regular practice of doing your fair share, and not taking more than your fair share, is a large part of family etiquette. Sharing comes into play in many important ways, including the following situations:

- **Using the bathroom:** When bathrooms serve more than one person, and when a number of family members need to make themselves presentable for the day ahead, the etiquette of sharing space requires that you use the bathroom for only your fair share of time. If need be, set up a bathroom schedule, giving everyone the same amount of time — that way, each person can count on getting the bathroom to himself during his allotted time slot.

- **Housekeeping:** You can do a great favor for future daughters-in-law and sons-in-law by teaching your kids to pick up after themselves and to do their fair share of the general housekeeping. Straightening a bed, putting dirty clothing into the hamper, placing dirty dishes in the dishwasher or rinsing them off in the sink, and putting away personal possessions before retiring for the night takes only an extra minute or two — and these are all chores your kids can help out with.

- **Counting the cupcakes:** When four adults sit down to a pie sliced into four pieces, it's clear that everyone will get one piece. Put four children in front of a dessert tray of four cupcakes, however, and the results are not as obvious. Children need to be taught how to measure objects — particularly desirable objects such as cupcakes — with their eyes and calculate their fair share.

Talking to Your Children about People with Disabilities

Many children already know a person with a disability, perhaps a grandparent or a classmate at school. Use these experiences as a springboard for discussion. Explain that people of all ages have disabilities and why (an accident, an illness, or simply the way the person was born). Let your children know that having a disability is okay, a fact of life. Point out all the things that people with disabilities can do.

Some children, if given inadvertent free rein, will walk up to a person with a disability, tug on his or her sleeve, and say, "You look funny." The proclamation isn't so much a judgment as a statement of fact, a result of the child's curiosity about the world.

Make sure that your child knows that saying or doing anything that may hurt a person's feelings is never okay. At the same time, don't discourage his or her natural curiosity. The worst thing you can tell a child — unless you first explain why — is not to stare. Doing so is as good as saying, "Let's pretend the person with crutches doesn't exist."

If your child is curious about a person's wheelchair — or her white cane, or his life — explain that asking questions is okay, but that it's also okay if the person doesn't really want to talk. If possible, make eye contact with the person who has the disability. If he or she seems receptive to your child, approach, let the child say, "Could I ask you a question?" and see what happens. Many people with disabilities are very willing to respond to children's questions, especially because a child's reaction to the answer is likely to be, "Oh, neat." No discomfort, no fear.

 If children today feel at ease around people with disabilities, adults tomorrow will feel the same way. You want your children to be polite. If they happen to grow up to make the world a better place, that's an added bonus.

Part 4

Health and Safety

This part is dedicated to things you can do to keep your kids healthy and safe.

When it comes to your children's good health, you need to do things — like instill healthy habits in your kids, keep the spread of germs to a minimum, protect your kids from the elements, and keep your medicine cabinet well stocked — to prevent trips to the doctor. You also need to do your part to prevent serious illnesses before they occur by scheduling regular checkups for your children. In addition, because your kids will inevitably get sick, you need to know how to deal with common illnesses and how to reassure your kids that doctors are there to help.

When it comes to your children's safety, know that nothing is more important than being organized and prepared. You need to teach your kids how to be safe — at home and abroad. You also need to know how to avoid accidents and how to prevent and deal with substance abuse.

Chapter 14

Preventing Trips to the Doctor

As a parent, you're charged with keeping your kids healthy by helping them avoid the things that make them sick. Doing so requires effort and common sense, both of which seem to be lacking when it comes to a kid's regular mode of operation.

This chapter is dedicated to things you can do to prevent trips to the doctor.

Developing Healthy Habits

Developing healthy habits for your family keeps them safe and free from illness. Do the following, and you just may turn them into habits that stay with your children the rest of their lives:

🌸 **Practice proper nutrition.** Eat three meals a day and two snacks, limiting high-sugar and high-fat foods and pushing fruits, vegetables, meats, and dairy products. (See Chapter 6 for details on establishing healthy eating habits.)

🌸 **Be smart with your food.** Wash fruits and vegetables and don't eat undercooked meats or poultry. (See Chapter 6 for additional tips.)

🌸 **Make sure everyone in the family is getting regular exercise.** (See Chapter 6 for details on making fitness part of your family's everyday lives.)

🌸 **Go to bed and get enough sleep.** (See Chapter 7 for details.)

☺ ☻ ☹ ☺ ☺ ☹ ☺ ☺ ☹ ☺ ☺ ☹ ☺ ☺ ☹ ☺ ☺ ☺ ☹ ☺

❀ **Visit your doctor for regular well-child exams and keep up to date on all the recommended vaccines.** (See Chapter 15 for details.)

❀ **Have emergency phone numbers by your phone.** (See Chapter 16 for other safety precautions.)

❀ **Pay positive attention to your child.** (See Chapter 4 for details.)

❀ **Turn off the television and read a book or play a game.** (See Chapter 4 for related tips.)

❀ **Teach the dangers of drugs, tobacco, and alcohol.** (See Chapter 16 for details.)

Preventing the Spread of Germs

Germs *rarely* are spread by flying through the air with the greatest of ease. They're transferred by hands or by some sort of touching. Keeping this in mind, follow these suggestions on how to restrict the spread of germs:

❀ **Don't share towels.** Especially avoid towel-sharing if you dry off one child with a runny nose and then need to dry off your other children.

❀ **Don't share cups.** Sure, giving your child a drink from your cup is an easy habit to fall into, but try to avoid this type of sharing as much as possible. You can designate a cup for each family member to use for an entire day. That way you're not using every cup in the house, but you're also not sharing each other's coughs and colds.

❀ **Don't kiss your pets.** As much as you love your pet cats, dogs, iguanas, or whatever, reserve your affection to petting and giving them proper care. Save the kissing for your family. Pets carry around germs, and you don't want to get anything that they have.

❀ **Don't sit on a dirty toilet seat.** Toilet seats can be pretty nasty. That's why someone developed those paper gaskets to sit on in public restrooms.

❀ **Don't eat raw meat or eggs.** Raw meat and eggs carry bacteria.

❀ **Don't smoke.** Secondhand smoke increases the amount and severity of colds, coughs, ear infections, and respiratory problems in those around you. If you smoke around your kids, they're smoking, too.

❀ **Don't touch your face.** Although it's a hard lesson to teach, little hands must be kept off little faces. Consider the following basic math problem: touching a runny nose + wiping something out of your eye = an eye infection.

❀ **Do teach your kids to sneeze or cough in the right place.** The rule is not to cover your face with your hands when you sneeze or cough, but rather to cover your face with the bend of your arm. Sneezing into your hand and then grabbing the door handle means you're giving your germs to the door handle (which will then be touched by someone else). Sneeze into your arm instead.

❀ **Do wash your hands.** And wash everyone else's hands, too. Wash hands after using the bathroom, after changing a diaper, after sneezing or coughing, before and after handling food, before you eat, after working in dirt, and after cleaning. Wash your children's hands before and after they eat, after they go potty, if they grab themselves during a diaper change, after they play with friends, when they get home from school or daycare, and whenever you see them wiping or rubbing their eyes or nose.

❀ **Do disinfect your house often.** Disinfecting your home is a lifelong process. Wash everything, including doorknobs, anything and everything in your kitchen, and anything to do with your children — like toys and diaper-changing supplies.

Taking Precautions against the Elements

The sun, heat, and cold are harmful elements if you don't correctly prepare for them. Your children have very delicate skin, and those elements affect them more than they would you (someone whose skin has aged and been weathered, kind of like a really comfortable saddle).

Sun protection

If it's a nice, sunny day, your kids are going to want to be outside — and they should be. The sun is a great source of vitamin D. But like most things in life, the sun is good only in moderation. Take these precautions:

❀ **Avoid letting your children go out into the sun between the hours of 10:00 a.m. and 3:00 p.m.** This is the time of day when the sun is the strongest. It's hottest during this time, too, and the sun can do more damage to the delicate skin of a child.

❀ **Keep hats on your children if they're going to be in the sun.** A hat not only protects a child's skin from the sun, but it also keeps the head cooler, which, in turn, helps the child avoid sunstroke.

❀ **Use sunscreen on your children any time they're going to be in the sun (except for babies younger than 6 months old — they shouldn't be in the sun at all).** This also means winter sun. Use a sunscreen with SPF 15 or higher (SPF stands for *sun protection factor*) — one that says it is waterproof and *hypoallergenic*, or non-irritating. These types of sunscreens won't have heavy perfumes in them and will be gentler for delicate skin.

☺ ☺ ☹ ☺ ☺ ☹ ☺ ☺ ☹ ☺ ☺ ☹ ☺ ☺ ☹ ☺ ☺ ☺ ☹ ☺

- **Apply sunscreen on all body parts that are exposed to the sun.** This includes ears, noses, backs of hands, and backs of necks. You'll also want to use a lip balm with sunscreen so that your little ones don't get burned or chapped lips from the sun and wind.

- **Lubricate your children with sunscreen liberally and often.** Really smear it on well. But don't apply sunscreen near the eyes — it can be very irritating. Read the directions on your sunscreen, too. You'll find that you'll have to reapply it often — especially if they're swimming or running through sprinklers. One slathering is never enough.

The sun will burn a child's skin from reflective surfaces. That means water and snow. And a common mistake made by parents is forgetting that the sun can be more harmful and stronger than they think it is. Nine out of ten skin *melanomas* (cancers) are linked to severe sunburn during childhood.

Sunburns actually are mild, first-degree burns. When your kids get sunburned, make a compress of equal parts chilled milk and cold water. Apply the compress to their lips and eyelids to relieve the swollen, hot feeling. Cooled tea bags placed on the skin also help relieve sunburn. Give acetaminophen (for example, Tylenol) or ibuprofen (for example, Advil) for a few days to help with the pain. Use a moisturizer and a 1 percent hydrocortisone cream three times a day. And don't forget to give your sunburned child plenty of fluids to drink.

Heat protection

Adults feel that first drop of sweat, and we're running in to air-conditioning or off to the shade. But kids will play forever in the sun without complaining. For some reason, kids just don't know temperatures.

To help your kids enjoy warm weather, follow some basic safety rules:

- **When it's hot outside, keep a close eye on your kids.** If they appear too hot (red-faced, sweating, looking pale or faint), bring them in and cool them down.

- **Don't let your kids stay outside for more than an hour at a time without having them cool down.**

- **Provide your kids with plenty of liquids.** Cool water is the best thing you can give them on a hot day.

Staying in the heat too long causes heatstroke; the body is unable to cool itself. And children can suffer from heatstroke just as easily as adults. They commonly have strokes when they play outside in the heat for too long and when they're overdressed for the heat. If you think your child may have heatstroke, call for help immediately, move her to a cool place, and — starting with the head — sponge her down with cool water (not ice water or rubbing alcohol). With heatstroke comes dehydration, so start giving your child cool liquids, too.

Cold protection (as in weather, not the sniffles)

The best way to spend winter is inside, nestled in a big, overstuffed chair, sitting by a big roaring fire, and drinking hot peppermint tea with a bag of Oreos on the side. Okay, so that's *one* opinion. Children think differently. As is true of the heat, children don't seem to mind the cold. And they can become overexposed to the cold, so be sure to do the following:

- ❋ **Never send your kids outside in the cold without proper clothing.** That means long underwear, turtlenecks, water-repellent long pants, water-repellent coats and shoes, heavy cotton socks, hats that cover the ears, and mittens that are lined and waterproof (they'll keep your children's hands warmer than gloves).

- ❋ **Keep children's fingers and toes dry when they play outdoors in cold weather.** Buy waterproof clothing! Wet clothing makes skin cold and increases the risk of frostbite (see the nearby sidebar "Looking for signs of frostbite").

- ❋ **Make sure boots and other winter shoes are not too tight.** Tight footwear affects the circulation and can lead to frostbite.

- ❋ **Limit the time your children spend outdoors.** When the weather is windy or rainy, when the temperature is below 32° F, or when the wind chill reaches 0° F or below, limit the exposure time.

The cold air of winter can cause children's faces to become chapped. To prevent chapping, apply moisturizing cream to their faces before they go out. If they have a runny nose, put petroleum jelly under their noses and on their chins. Petroleum jelly won't wash off as easily as moisturizing cream.

Looking for signs of frostbite

Listen to your kids whenever they say they're getting cold. Bring them inside and look for these signs of frostbite:

* Their skin feels very cold, and they've lost feeling in that area.
* Their skin is pale, glossy, and hard.

Note: If you think your child has frostbite, call your doctor immediately.

To help with frostbite, give your child warm liquids to drink and put her in warm water to start bringing warmth back into the frostbitten area. (Be careful of the water, though, because it will feel warmer to a frostbitten child than it actually is.) You may also try warming your child by wrapping her in blankets or putting the affected area in a warm washcloth or heated towel. *Don't rub the affected area.* Rubbing not only is painful but also can damage the skin.

As your child begins warming up, her skin may feel like it's burning or tingling, and it should start turning red. You can't do anything about that burning feeling, except try to comfort her.

Knowing What to Keep in the Medicine Cabinet

The time will come when your children do catch colds or the flu — or, for that matter, use their heads to stop the floor. Be prepared to take care of minor things. Keeping a well-stocked medicine cabinet may just help prevent a trip to the doctor.

 When in doubt about whether something is minor, always call the doctor. Don't take chances with your kids' health.

Use the following checklist for supplies to keep on hand for minor problems:

* **Thermometer:** Those that you stick in the armpit and in the ear (and they're two different kinds) are fairly accurate and easy to use.

* **Eyedropper:** Children occasionally get eye infections along with a cold. They rub their faces and smear germs all over, including into their eyes. Eyedroppers are good for dropping mild saltwater into a child's eye to help clear up the infection.

🙂 🙂 🙂 🙂 🙂 🙂 🙂 🙂 🙂 🙂 🙂 🙂 🙂 🙂 🙂 🙂 🙂 🙂 🙂 🙂

❋ **Medicine dispenser:** You'll need something to give out medicine. Drug stores usually have a dispenser that looks like a large spoon with measurements on the side (see Figure 14-1). Remember to clean the medicine dispenser after every use.

❋ **Children's pain reliever:** Use only acetaminophen (Tylenol is one brand) or ibuprofen (Advil, for example) when your doctor recommends it. Keep in mind that this medicine should be used sparingly, and only when your children have considerable discomfort from a cold or flu. Tylenol, or any medicines of the same nature, won't cure colds or the flu. Their only purpose is to hide the symptoms of an infection and make your children feel better.

❋ **Ice packs:** Gravity and your children will become well acquainted. The end result will be several bumps on the head and a few bloody lips. Those are the times when you need an ice pack. You can buy ice packs that you keep in your freezer, or you can make one by putting ice and cold water in a baggy and wrapping it in a washcloth. Never put ice directly on a child's skin. Not only does it hurt when you do this, but you can also damage the skin. *Warning:* If your child gets a deep cut, put an ice pack on the cut and go to the doctor. Doctors are better equipped for this kind of injury.

❋ **Adhesive bandages:** If your child falls and skins a knee, the best thing to do is wash the cut with soap and water and then leave it alone. It's better for cuts to be open to the air. But sometimes kids won't leave a cut alone. That's when you'll need an adhesive bandage (Band-Aid is one brand). Put the bandage on loosely so that the cut can still get some air.

❋ **Petroleum jelly:** This stuff is for chapped lips or faces, to put under runny noses so your kids' faces don't get sore from wiping their noses, to prevent diaper rash, and for those ever-so-popular rectal thermometers.

❋ **Lip balm:** Whenever your children catch a cold, their lips are likely to become chapped, because they're breathing through their mouths. If lips become too chapped, they'll crack and bleed, so keep those tender little lips nice and lubed.

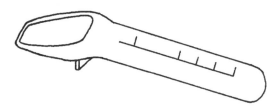

Figure 14-1: This tool makes the medicine go down almost as well as a spoonful of sugar.

☺ ☹ ☺ ☺ ☺ ☹ ☺ ☺ ☹ ☺ ☺ ☹ ☺ ☺ ☹ ☺ ☺ ☺ ☹ ☺

- **Anti-itch lotion:** This lotion is for when your children become the main course for hungry mosquitoes. It's also good for rashes, insect bites, and poison ivy.

- **Syrup of Ipecac:** You give this syrup when your children swallow something poisonous. *Warning:* Give Syrup of Ipecac to your child only if you have been instructed to do so by your doctor or the Poison Control Center.

- **Flashlight or penlight:** These items are for looking down sore throats as well as removing splinters.

- **Moisturizing soap and lotion:** Lotion is especially needed during the winter months when skin tends to dry out. Don't use lotions on children too often during the summer, because it only makes them feel hot.

- **Tweezers:** These are a definite must for pulling out splinters.

- **Cool-mist humidifier or vaporizer:** This type of vaporizer (even if you *can't* fit it in your medicine cabinet) is great for when your children have colds. The cool, moist air is easier to breathe than dry, warm air. It also loosens the mucus in their noses. You must clean the humidifier daily so that it doesn't get moldy.

- **Scissors:** Use these for cutting bandages, gauze, or tape to size. Keep a small pair of scissors in your medicine cabinet so that you don't have to go hunting for a pair when you need them.

Chapter **15**

Visiting Dr. Everything'll-Be-All-Right

When it comes to your child's good health, visiting the doctor is a key component. You need to do your part to prevent serious illnesses before they occur by scheduling regular checkups for your child. In addition, showing your child that doctors (or other medical professionals) are for helping is up to you, so you need to instill in your child that no matter how much doctors poke, prod, and stick, they're trying to make her feel better. And, of course, it's also important that you know what to do when your child does get sick because, alas, it's inevitable — she will.

Establishing a Positive Child/ Doctor Relationship

Your child looks to you to observe how you behave in situations. So setting a good example is up to you when taking your child to the doctor. The example you want to set is that you think the doctor is a good person even though he or she may do things that hurt or are uncomfortable, such as administering shots, sticking cold things on your chest, flashing lights in your eyes, and probing in your ears. Your child needs to know it's all for a good purpose.

Keep these rules in mind when going to the doctor:

* **Be happy and relaxed.** If you're relaxed and comfortable, your child will be more relaxed.

* **Greet the doctor cheerfully.** Doing so lets your child know that the doctor is a person you like and are happy to see.

* **Use the doctor's name.** People seem more like friends when you address them by name. This practice also teaches your child the name of the doctor.

* **Thank the doctor after the examination.** This strategy again reinforces to your child the fact that the doctor is someone who is here to help.

* **Don't use going to the doctor as a threat against your child.** Avoid saying "If you aren't good, I'll take you to the doctor for a shot." The next time your child has to go to the doctor, the kid's going to feel in trouble for something and be worried the whole time about getting a shot.

* **Don't tell your child that something is going to hurt, or that it won't hurt if you really know that it will.** The best thing to do is keep quiet and let your child decide whether it hurts.

Scheduling Regular Checkups

Regular checkups keep kids healthy. Your child's doctor monitors general growth (height, weight, head size, and so on), evaluates emotional and physical health, and administers immunizations.

Usually, parents schedule the most visits in a child's lifetime during the child's early years. In fact, you may feel like you're living at the doctor's office (new parents especially feel this way). But take heart: The number of visits drops greatly as your child ages (see the next section for proof).

Immunizations

Immunizations, inoculations, or shots are a fact of life for kids, and mostly a healthy one at that. Shots protect your youngster from diseases that interfere big-time with learning. Particles in the shot serums activate the body's normal network of antibodies to fight off any other intrusion of that particular bug. Today, many diseases, such as polio and measles, are rare thanks to immunization.

Prepare for your child to receive about 20 shots recommended by the American Academy of Pediatrics before entering kindergarten (see Table 15-1). Most occur within the first two years of life, which is good.

Chances are slim to none that your chicklet will remember as an adult the torture you put her through.

Table 15-1 Checkup and Immunization Schedule

Age for Checkup	Immunizations	Checkup
Newborn		General evaluation on ten-point scale
2 to 4 weeks	Hepatitis B	General evaluation
2 months	Hepatitis B (1 to 4 months) DtaP (diphtheria, tetanus, lockjaw, pertussis) Polio, pneumonia/meningitis Hib (Influenza type b)	General evaluation
4 months	DtaP Hib Polio Pneumonia	General evaluation
6 months	Hepatitis B (6 to 18 months) DtaP Hib Polio (6 to 18 months) Pneumonia	General evaluation
9 months		General evaluation
12 months	Hib (booster 12 to 15 months) Pneumonia (12 to 15 months) MMR (measles, mumps, rubella; 12 to 15 months) Varicella (chicken pox; 12 to 18 months)	General evaluation
15 months	DtaP (15 to 18 months)	General evaluation
18 months		General evaluation
2 years	Hepatitis A (if recommended)	General evaluation
3 years		General evaluation
4 years	DtaP (4 to 6 years) Polio (4 to 6 years) MMR (4 to 6 years)	General evaluation
5, 6, 8, 10 years		General evaluation
11 to 21, yearly	Td (Tetanus and diphtheria only: 11 to 16 years; boosters every ten years thereafter)	General evaluation

147

You may question the amount of times your child acts as a pincushion. But she won't be able to go to school without most inoculations. Most shots are safe, or, at the very least, their benefits outweigh the small reactions some kids experience.

 You may want to touch base with folks who keep track of the latest research into the safety of vaccines to know which ones trigger reactions more frequently. Contact the National Vaccine Information Center at 421 East Church Street, Suite 206, Vienna, VA 22180; phone: 800-909-SHOT; or Internet: www.909shot.com.

If you'd like a handy place to track the checkup/immunization schedule of your child, use Table 15-2 (and feel free to make copies if you have more than one child). Write your child's name in the space provided at the top, record the date of the checkup/immunization, and jot down notes and/or any shot reactions.

Table 15-2 Checkup and Immunization Schedule of _____

Age for Checkup	Immunizations	Date	Notes/Reactions
Newborn		_____	_____ _____ _____
2–4 weeks	Hepatitis B	_____	_____ _____ _____
2 months	Hepatitis B (1 to 4 months)	_____	_____ _____
	DtaP (diphtheria, tetanus, lockjaw, pertussis)	_____	_____ _____ _____
	Polio, pneumonia/ meningitis	_____	_____ _____ _____
	Hib (Influenza type b)	_____	_____ _____ _____

☺ ☺ ☹ ☺ ☺ ☹ ☺ ☺ ☹ ☺ ☺ ☹ ☺ ☺ ☹ ☺ ☺ ☹ ☺

Age for Checkup	Immunizations	Date	Notes/Reactions
4 months	DtaP	_____	_____
	Hib	_____	_____
	Polio	_____	_____
	Pneumonia	_____	_____
6 months	Hepatitis B (6 to 18 months)	_____	_____
	DtaP	_____	_____
	Hib	_____	_____
	Polio (6 to 18 months)	_____	_____
	Pneumonia	_____	_____
9 months		_____	_____
12 months	Hib (booster 12 to 15 months)	_____	_____
	Pneumonia (12 to 15 months)	_____	_____
	MMR (measles, mumps, rubella; 12 to 15 months)	_____	_____

continued

☺ ☺ ☹ ☺ ☺ ☹ ☺ ☺ ☹ ☺ ☺ ☹ ☺ ☺ ☹ ☺ ☺ ☺ ☺ ☹ ☺

Table 15-2 Checkup and Immunization Schedule of _____ (continued)

Age for Checkup	Immunizations	Date	Notes/Reactions
	Varicella (chicken pox; 12 to 18 months)	_____	_____
15 months	DtaP (15 to 18 months)	_____	_____
18 months		_____	_____
2 years	Hepatitis A (if recommended)	_____	_____
3 years		_____	_____
4 years	DtaP (4 to 6 years)	_____	_____
	Polio (4 to 6 years)	_____	_____
	MMR (4 to 6 years)	_____	_____
5, 6, 8, 10 years		_____	_____
11 to 21, yearly	Td (Tetanus and diphtheria only: 11 to 16 years; boosters every ten years thereafter)	_____	_____

Vision

Taking care of your child's vision is an important part of preventive health care. Babies' eyes are examined in the newborn nursery at the hospital and by a doctor during the 6-month and later well-baby visits. Your regular physician checks for muscle problems and infections.

Your child's school should offer evaluations upon registering. In addition, you need to make an appointment for your child to visit an ophthalmologist between the ages of 3 and 4, and then every year following that.

 Take your child for regular eye checkups to make sure she sees well. Kids often can't express why they can't see the blackboard or why they hold objects up to their noses to investigate them.

No matter what the age of your child, make an appointment with your doctor if any of the following happens:

- Your child squints or rubs his eyes a lot (other than when tired).
- Your child's eyes move quickly either up or down or from side to side.
- Your child's eyes are watery, sensitive to light, or look different from the way they normally do.
- Your child's eyes stay red for several days.
- Your child's eyelids droop, or the eyes look like they bulge.
- Sores or styes are on the eyelids.
- The pupil of the eye has white, grayish-white, or yellow-colored material in it.
- Pus or crust in either eye doesn't go away.
- One eye is turning in.
- Your child holds playthings and books close to the face.
- Your child blinks excessively.

Speech and hearing

Children can't learn language and social cues without the ability to hear clearly. At minimum, hearing loss affects the ability to learn how to talk.

 If you find that your child is at risk for hearing loss, don't panic. Even if your child shows some hearing loss early on, she can shine with her peers by the time school starts if the loss is picked up and corrected early.

After an initial hearing screening at 3 months of age (if your maternity center didn't screen when your child was a newborn), check your baby's hearing every six months until age 3. After that, screen at the following times:

❀ When entering school

❀ Every year from kindergarten through third grade

❀ In seventh grade

❀ In eleventh grade

❀ Any time your child shows learning problems that may indicate the need for special-education classes or grade retention

Teeth

When you take your child on regular visits to the doctor, he or she will check the development of your child's teeth. In addition, you can try taking your child to a dentist as a toddler.

Getting your children on a regular, every-six-months checkup schedule is important. And you need to develop the same kind of open, trusting relationship with your dentist that you have with your pediatrician. Your children need to know that a dentist is someone who makes sure their teeth are healthy, strong, and growing well.

 When you have a concern about your children's teeth, don't wait. If your children start to develop brown spots or places where it looks like teeth are beginning to rot, if their gums are swollen or they bleed during brushing, or if their gums or teeth hurt, make an appointment right away.

 Did you know that the American Dental Association recommends introducing your child to a dentist within six months after the first tooth appears? The thinking is that your child gets used to the dentist and starts on the right track for cleaning and flossing. That way, she never has to face the drill or pain of tooth decay later on, which sounds great, doesn't it?

Dealing with Illness

The time will come when your child gets sick — regardless of how diligently you schedule those regular checkups to keep him healthy. This section points out some signs that indicate your child may be sick and provides some basic advice on how to deal with three common child illnesses: colds, fevers, and ear infections.

Resources for illnesses

An easy-to-follow comprehensive source for healthcare guidelines is *Your Child's Health: The Parent's Guide to Symptoms, Emergencies, Common Illnesses, Behavior, and School Problems* by Barton Schmitt. Parents like this book because it identifies symptoms and illnesses, indicates when to call the doctor, and simplifies the process with its A-B-C instructions. But, as with other far-reaching medical tomes, this one falls short on general parenting philosophy, so take that information lightly.

To connect with humans for information, contact the American Academy of Pediatrics, 141 Northwest Point Road, Elk Grove Village, IL 60009; phone: 800-433-9016; Internet: www.aap.org.

Signs that your child may be sick

Young kids often can't tell you why they lack enthusiasm for exploration. If they can talk at all, they can tell you only that they hurt or feel "yucky." Older kids don't want to miss out on what's going on at school or some after-school activity. Or they feign illness as a way to get out of something, such as a test they never studied for. So you have to play detective and look for these signs of physical distress:

* Orneriness or weepiness

* Prolonged sleeping during the day

* Other changes in sleeping schedules or difficulty in waking up from sleep

* Not eating as much as normal

* Change in skin color (pale green, gray, yellow, and pasty white are signs something isn't right)

* Dark circles under the eyes, blue lips, acting limp, and lacking any energy

* Bloodshot or runny eyes, dilated pupils

* Rubbing a part of the body, such as the stomach, head, or ears

* Favoring one side of the body over another, such as with feet or hands

* Screaming loudly with knees drawn up

* Fever above 101° F

☺ ☻ ☹ ☺ ☺ ☹ ☺ ☺ ☹ ☺ ☺ ☹ ☺ ☺ ☹ ☺ ☺ ☺ ☺ ☹ ☺

- ✿ Difficulty breathing
- ✿ Swollen glands
- ✿ Bad breath
- ✿ Smelly private parts even after a bath

Never take cranky behavior, low fevers, or any other unusual behavior too lightly, because it may mean that an illness is developing or an infection is brewing somewhere. Get your kid to the doctor; don't ever take chances on your child's health.

Sniffles and sneezes

When your child gets a cold, you'll wonder who feels worse — you or your child. You feel bad because there isn't really a whole lot you can do for someone who has a cold. And your child feels bad because that's what colds do to people.

When you notice the sniffles and sneezes coming on, immediately start to work on:

- ✿ **Washing doorknobs and toys that can be handled by other children.** Germs are transferred mainly by hands, and you don't want anyone else getting sick.

- ✿ **Washing your and your children's hands every chance that you get.** You don't want to catch the cold, and you don't want to pass it on to someone else. You also don't want your children rubbing snotty noses and then rubbing their eyes, spreading germs all over the place. That's how eye colds or eye infections begin.

- ✿ **Being prepared to give your doctor a detailed description of your children's symptoms.** Can you describe how your children are acting, eating, and feeling? What their bowel movements are like? If they're pulling at their ears? Coughing and producing anything (and what it looks like)? If their noses are running? And what color (clear or green) the stuff coming out is?

Fevers

Fevers are a sign that the body has an infection, such as a cold or flu. You can do nothing to make a fever disappear other than healing the body to make the infection go away. Medications such as acetaminophen will reduce the fever, but they won't cure the problem.

☺ ☺ ☹ ☺ ☺ ☹ ☺ ☺ ☹ ☺ ☺ ☹ ☺ ☺ ☹ ☺ ☺ ☹ ☺

Ask your pediatrician about giving your child acetaminophen (like children's Tylenol). And always ask your doctor about brand names, amounts of medicine, and appropriate times to give it *before* giving your child any medication.

 Never, ever give your child aspirin unless your doctor has prescribed it. When given to children (up to about 19 years old), aspirin can cause Reye's Syndrome, a rare disorder that may result in coma or even death.

When your child has a fever, she has an infection somewhere, and that usually means your child is contagious. So wash your hands as often as possible until the fever is gone. Germs are passed by the hands, and you don't want whatever is making your child sick to make you sick — and you don't want to pass it on to other family members.

Ear infections

Suffering ear infections and never seeming to be able to get rid of them is a sad fact about many babies and small children. Their ear canals are small, which can trap liquid and lead to an infection.

Your doctor can prescribe medication for ear infections that should clear them up within seven to ten days. Always go back to the doctor for the recommended checkup, because these infections aren't always easy to clear up. Lingering infections are common and can cause damage.

Don't take ear infections lightly, because they can lead to other, more harmful problems. Whenever you find your child pulling at an ear, take her to the doctor. Children with ear infections may also be irritable, run a fever, or have other signs of illness.

 Be wary of doctors who suggest that you have tubes put in your child's ears, especially when the suggestion comes on the first visit for an ear infection. In some children, tubes help decrease infections, but this solution isn't always necessary. Get a second opinion.

If You're in the Market for a Doctor

Are you currently without a doctor but in the market for one? Use the questionnaire in Table 15-3 as a guideline to finding the right doctor for your family.

☺ ☺ ☹ ☺ ☺ ☹ ☺ ☺ ☹ ☺ ☺ ☹ ☺ ☺ ☹ ☺ ☺ ☺ ☹ ☺

Table 15-3 Questionnaire for Doctor Hunting

Question	Answer
What are your open hours?	
How do you handle follow-up visits?	
Do you have bench checks or less expensive follow-up visits?	❏ Yes ❏ No
What are my payment options?	
What do I do in case of an emergency?	
Do you have additional doctors in your practice?	❏ Yes ❏ No
Do you have backup doctors available when you're away?	❏ Yes ❏ No
How is your waiting room arranged?	

Chapter 16

Keeping Your Child Safe (In a World That Isn't Always)

In This Chapter

☺ Teaching toddlers how to be safe

☺ Keeping children safe at home

☺ Avoiding accidents

☺ Preventing and dealing with substance abuse

Nothing is more important than being organized and prepared for safety issues regarding your children. This chapter helps you do just that by teaching your kids basic safety rules and making your home and children's environment safe.

Teaching Safety Basics to Toddlers

Smart older kids are safe kids. They know how to avoid dangerous situations. But even if she's so inclined, you can't count on your toddler/preschooler to understand danger yet. Kids this age are naturally erratic, excitable, and impatient — and that's a bad combination. They run into streets after balls. They hide inside clothing racks in stores. And they may even go with a friendly adult they meet at the mall. Even when you plan on always staying together, your child may disappear when you turn your head or become involved in a conversation.

As a parent, you do the best you can. That involves beginning to train early for situations you hope will never happen. At this age, your child won't miraculously understand the first time around what throws you into a tailspin. In your child's egocentric manner (which is perfectly normal), she assumes you exist to serve and take care of her, keeping all harm away.

You don't want to scare your little person so much that she never leaves your side. But you can begin to work on the basics of who and what constitute danger. Teach your child to

❀ **Stay away from water's edge.** Review pool and beach rules before each outing. (Check out the section "Swimming do's," later in this chapter, for other safety tips.)

❀ **Understand fire safety.** (For some specific tips, see the nearby "Hot fire-safety tips for tots" sidebar.)

❀ **Play where you can see her.** Make sure she knows to ask you or a caregiver before going somewhere or with someone else.

❀ **Pay attention when you talk.** Don't get in the habit of repeating what you want a dozen times until your child acts. She'll learn to tune you out. And safety-related directions usually need immediate responses. So make directions clear, with understandable consequences for not responding after one time.

❀ **Talk with you about anyone who approaches her;** wants to give her something tempting, such as a puppy, money, or candy; offers her a ride; hangs around the playground; or asks her to keep a secret. Emphasize the importance of never getting close to someone else's car without permission, no matter how tempting.

❀ **Go to the nearest checkout counter, security officer, or lost and found if she gets separated from you while shopping or in a public place.** When going to a large store or mall, point out whom your child can trust, in case you get separated or there's an emergency. Take time for a couple run-throughs before heading off to do your chores together.

❀ **Cross the street safely.** Practice street crossing together. Toddlers are *not* ready to cross independently yet. But you can begin pointing out the fine points of successful street crossing, such as crossing at the corner, looking both ways before leaving the curb, knowing streetlight etiquette (red means stop and green means go, as well as the character symbol for walk and the hand symbol for stop), walking and riding bicycles on sidewalks only, and going places with a buddy.

In addition, make sure your toddler/preschooler knows the following street-smart information:

❀ **Name (first and last), address, and phone number (with area code).**

❀ **Parents' names (first and last rather than Mommy and Daddy).**

❀ **Body parts.** Teach your kids where their private parts are and what names you want them to be called. Stress that parts covered by a swimsuit are considered private. Also talk about appropriate and inappropriate touching. Stress that no one should touch your kids' private parts other than a doctor during an exam or a parent when necessary (such as when bathing them or examining them when they're hurt or sick). Let your kids know that if someone asks to see or touch them in any way they don't like, they won't get in trouble, but they need to tell you right away. In addition, teach your kids how to shake hands with friends or relatives they don't want to kiss.

Remember: Many parents have no trouble discussing dangers such as kidnapping with their children, but they hesitate to discuss appropriate and inappropriate touching. It really is the same concept: You know certain dangers exist in the world, and although you don't want to make your kids paranoid, you do want to give them all the necessary information to keep themselves safe.

- **That 911 is what you dial during an emergency.** Make sure she knows how to use rotary and push-button telephones and can dial "0" for operator at a pay phone.

Ensuring Safety around the House

To ensure safety around the house, the best thing to do is look at each room from a child's point of view. Go ahead and sit on the floor to see what a child sees. Try to be as critical of the room as you possibly can. Is there anything that can hurt a child, or anything that she can get into or put into her mouth that she shouldn't?

Hot fire-safety tips for tots

Children under age 5 are at the greatest risk during fires. But fire safety takes practice. Start giving your preschooler the following fire-safety messages now:

- Stay away from items that cause intense heat and flames, such as matches and candles.
- Always give matches and lighters you find to an adult.
- Never touch hot appliances, such as oven burners and space heaters.
- Know the sound of a smoke alarm and tell an adult if it rings. If fire or smoke blocks your way to an adult, leave the house.
- If you go to a door and it feels hot, keep it closed and look for another way out.
- Crawl on the floor where air is clearer of smoke.
- Never hide to get away from fire or smoke. Stay low to breathe easier but where firefighters can find you.
- Stop, drop, and roll to put out clothes that are on fire.

Be sure to practice fire drills that role-play two safe ways to leave the house. Make sure your child knows where to meet your family safely away from the house, such as under the side tree or behind the garage, and stay away from the burning building after you're out. Let firefighters retrieve pets, if they can.

Safety issues for older children who are home alone

When children are in junior high school and beyond, they're sometimes left at home alone between the time school ends and the time parents finish working. If your children are home alone and a stranger calls and asks, "Is your mother home?" the child should always answer, "I'm sorry, but she can't come to the phone right now. May I have your name and number? I'll have her call you as soon as she's free." No further answers are necessary, even if the stranger presses for further information about what the mother is doing or when she will be free.

Practicing this technique with your child is a good idea. Call at a rehearsed time and push your child for information. Teach your children to be polite but firm.

When something happens to your children, you're not going to have the time to open a book and start reading about how to stop a lip from bleeding or treat a burn. Learn basic first aid and write down the number for the Poison Control Center now. Then you'll be prepared for the worst — whenever it happens.

Bedroom safety

This room can be scary when you think about it. Bedtime is probably the only time your child is going to be alone for any length of time. You want to be almost microscopic when looking at this room:

❀ Keep bedding simple — sheet and blanket, for example.

❀ Don't use pillows (until a child is 3 years old).

❀ Don't put toddler beds near blinds, drapes, or wall hangings with cords that hang down.

❀ Put plastic covers on all electrical outlets, and plastic boxes over the cords that are already plugged in.

❀ Make sure the toys in the bedroom are appropriate for the ages of your children.

❀ Wash and dry all toys on a regular basis. (Putting plastic toys in the dishwasher is a great way to disinfect them.)

❀ Don't put toy chests or children's furniture near windows.

☺ ☺ ☹ ☺ ☺ ☹ ☺ ☺ ☹ ☺ ☺ ☹ ☺ ☺ ☹ ☺ ☺ ☺ ☹ ☺

❀ Use toy chests made of light material, like plastic, with a lid that either comes off or hinges and stays up.

❀ Make sure purses and fanny packs are out of reach of children.

❀ Remove plastic covers from mattresses.

Living/family room safety

Because these are rooms where you and your family spend most of your time, you need to take extra precautions to make them safe:

❀ Put plastic covers on all the electrical outlets, and plastic boxes over the cords that are already plugged in.

❀ Put gates on all stairs going up or down. (Take portable gates to place in the doorways of staircases if you're traveling to someone else's home. Just be sure to ask for permission first.)

❀ Put breakable items either away or in higher places (until your children are old enough to learn to leave them alone).

❀ Don't leave young toddlers unattended on furniture.

❀ Scrape, sand, and repaint all old paint areas.

❀ Have furnaces, fireplaces, and gas grills checked for carbon monoxide leaks. Install a carbon-monoxide detector in your home.

❀ Clean air filters for heaters and air-conditioners once a month.

❀ Keep blind or drapery cords tied up, out of the reach of children.

Kitchen safety

Kitchens are one of the more dangerous places for your kids to hang out. Protect your children in the following ways:

❀ Put locks on all your cabinets.

❀ Use the back burners when cooking on the stove.

❀ Keep handles of pots turned toward the back of the stove. Never let them point out to where you're standing or where little hands can reach them.

❀ Keep drawers locked.

❀ Keep small children out of the way when cooking.

❀ Lock up or throw away plastic shopping bags, garbage bags, plastic wrap, plastic sandwich bags, plastic dry cleaning bags, or plastic film of any kind (like those on toy wrappings).

☺ ☺ ☹ ☺ ☺ ☹ ☺ ☺ ☹ ☺ ☺ ☹ ☺ ☺ ☹ ☺ ☺ ☺ ☹ ☺

- Keep alcoholic beverages away from children.
- Keep chairs away from counters.
- Keep important phone numbers on a list posted by the phone.
- Keep Syrup of Ipecac in your medicine cabinet, but don't use it unless you're instructed to do so by a physician or someone at the Poison Control Center.

Bathroom safety

Kids should not use the bathroom as a playroom. Your child can drown in only 1 inch of water, and your toilet has more than 1 inch of water in it. A baby who is old enough to reach into the toilet is old enough to fall in and drown. Keep the following bathroom safety tips in mind:

- Keep bathrooms blocked off with gates or install safety locks high enough so that your children can't reach them.
- Keep lids to toilets closed.
- Keep shower doors closed.
- Never leave water standing in sinks, bathtubs, or buckets.
- Keep cleaners, perfumes, deodorants, and such locked up.
- Always keep medicines in the medicine cabinet and away from children.
- Use child-resistant packaging for everything you use.
- Keep small appliances (like blow dryers, curling irons, and electric razors) unplugged and put away.
- Never leave children unattended in the bathroom, especially while they're taking a bath.

General fire-safety devices for the home

Look at the following list to see how well your house rates. If you don't have any of the following, get out that checkbook and go shopping!

- Smoke detectors
- Fire extinguishers
- Escape ladders
- Carbon-monoxide detectors
- A fire escape plan for your house that you practice regularly

Preventing Accidents

Accidents are one of the biggest reasons kids get hurt. Some of the falling down and bumps and bruises can't be helped. But kids also choke, get burned, and are cut for unnecessary reasons (as if there were good reasons to get choked, burned, and cut). You can take measures to prevent some of these accidents.

Burn prevention

Fire, hot objects, scalding liquids, and children do not mix. You want to do everything you can to avoid having to treat your child for burned fingers or worse. Cautionary measures are called for, so it's essential that you

- Put your coffee cup in the middle of tables or counters, not on the edge.
- Don't hold your children when you're holding a cup of hot liquid.
- Use your back burners to cook when possible.
- Turn pot handles toward the rear of the stove.
- Keep kids away from floor furnaces or area heaters.
- Hide your disposable lighters or don't use them.
- Don't let your children use the microwave oven.
- Never hold your children while you're cooking.

Choking hazards

Choking typically occurs in children because of how small their windpipes are. If your child is choking but still able to talk or cough, then she probably can handle the stuck item on her own.

 If she is unable to cough or talk, or if she turns blue, then she isn't getting any air to her lungs, and you need to help her right away. Call 911 immediately for help. In older children, you can perform the Heimlich maneuver, but this cannot be done to babies under 1 year of age. Attend a CPR class so that you can find out how to handle choking in children of all ages. Many hospitals offer free or significantly reduced prices for infant CPR classes.

Kids choke the most on the following items:

- Grapes
- Nuts
- Hard candies
- Popcorn
- Deflated or bursted balloon pieces
- Pins
- Coins
- Small toys and toy parts
- Raw vegetables cut in circles
- Hot dogs cut in circles
- Buttons
- Plastic bags

Playing don'ts

Don't put your kids in potentially dangerous places or areas, thinking that you'll keep a close eye on them. Kids can squirm around and move quicker than you can react. They can slip through your fingers before you know it.

Here are some other don'ts about playing:

- Don't let your kids ride on the lawn mower with you.
- Don't let your kids ride in the back of pickup trucks.
- Don't leave your kids on the edge of a swimming pool.
- Don't let your kids ride on four-wheelers, motorcycles, personal watercraft, or other recreational equipment when they're younger than the recommended age limit.

Unsafe toys are anything with plastic bags or cellophane wrappers. Children can easily choke on plastic and cellophane. Kids also like to put bags on their heads as pretend hats. Plastic bags over the head can cause suffocation.

 To find out how your playground stacks up, go to www.uni.edu/playground, the Web site of the National Program for Playground Safety, which rates your playground for safety.

164

Swimming do's

Water can be a scary thing, so keep these safety tips in mind:

❊ **Always supervise your children when they're around water of any type.** That means water in a bucket, a child's pool, or even big water puddles from rain.

❊ **Use swimming-pool safety.** Your pool should have a four-sided, 5-foot fence around it with a self-closing, self-latching gate.

❊ **Wait until your children are at least 3 years old before starting them in a swimming program.** The American Academy of Pediatrics (AAP) advises against infant swimming programs. They claim that babies can get parasitic infections from swimming pools. Babies can also swallow too much water, which leads to water intoxication. The AAP also believes that parents develop a false sense of security, thinking that their infants can swim.

❊ **Check to make sure your old spa, hot tub, or whirlpool is equipped with new, safer drain covers that the U.S. Consumer Product Safety Commission helped develop.** Hair entanglement and body-part entrapment have been known to cause drowning deaths in the older models of spas, hot tubs, and whirlpools. Have yours checked for safety.

 The saddest thing to hear is a parent who has lost a child to drowning say, "I was only gone for a minute."

Talking about Drugs, Alcohol, and Smoking

When your kids reach the age of 10 or so, you need to sit them down and have frank discussions about drugs, alcohol, and smoking. These discussions are uncomfortable for many parents, but as obnoxious as it is to think about, your children are being introduced to these subjects in elementary school. If you don't educate your children about these topics, you can count on the other kids at school teaching them (and not in the way you'd like).

 Studies show that the best way to prevent drug use is to monitor your teen's behavior. Kids with involved parents who set rules fend off pressures to mix with a risky crowd.

No matter what your teen says, you have a right and responsibility to know where she goes and with whom. You also have a responsibility to offset

bombardment of offensive media. To balance your desire to supervise your teen's behavior and your child's growing need for privacy and independence, see whether these alternatives strike a balance:

* Impose media guidelines that filter drug-infested influences.

* Explain in plain language how you feel about addictive substances.

* Institute a calling policy that makes sense so you know where your child is.

* Call a proposed sleepover or party house to confirm adult supervision.

* Stay alert to warning signs of a medical or substance-abuse problem.

* Talk regularly with your teen, and not just about logistics.

 At some point, almost every involved parent hears her teenager complain, "You don't trust me." Here's a great response to that teen mantra: "I trust you, but I don't want you to get into a situation you can't handle. So I'll be calling your friend's parents to make sure they're okay with having lots of kids over tonight."

The Columbia University CASA program administers www.casacolumbia.org for the National Center for Addiction and Abuse. The Web site's information covers the latest studies about substance abuse and what parents can do to keep healthy kids free of alcohol, tobacco, and drugs. Check it out. In addition:

* If your child is involved with drugs or alcohol, arrange a joint meeting with the school authorities and the law (if they're involved). Establish strict curfews. And if your child is addicted, seek the help of a therapist who may recommend in-patient rehabilitation care.

* If your child is smoking cigarettes, confront him. Ask for help from the school counselor, who may be able to offer you a quit-smoking program available through the school district. The American Lung Association, the American Heart Association, and the American Cancer Society also offer self-help programs for teens. Your family doctor can be a great help, as well.

 Secondhand smoke (smoke inhaled when someone else is smoking) is bad for your children and has been linked to premature babies, low-birth-weight babies, Sudden Infant Death Syndrome (SIDS), learning disabilities, and increased risk of asthma, pneumonia, and other medical problems. Even when you try to rationalize your smoking by saying that you only smoke outside, you have to realize that your children aren't stupid — they'll eventually realize what you're doing. Smoking anywhere, inside or outside the house, sets a bad example no matter how you look at it.

Ten Ways to Nurture Smart Kids

🌸 **Be willing to go the extra mile for each other.**
Make your family motto *family first.* Ensure that each person knows the important role he or she plays in the family and understands that this role sometimes involves pitching in and making sacrifices to strengthen family life.

🌸 **Respect each other.**
Listen without judging and act courteously and politely toward all kinds and ages of people, and chances are that your child will get the message that others deserve respect.

🌸 **Delight in each other.**
Enjoy each other and thrill at experiencing enriching adventures together. Read, listen to music, and play indoor and outdoor games together. Spend downtime together as well.

🌸 **Communicate with each other.**
As much as humanly possible given each family member's qualities, let every family member know that he or she is understood, and that his or her feelings and thoughts count.

🌸 **Grow from each other and from mistakes.**
Share your wisdom *with* your kids and, in addition, learn *from* your kids.

🌸 **Value effort, not product.**
Let your child know through actions and words what's really important. Being smart is about feeling good about yourself for doing the best you can.

🌸 **Solve problems together.**
Involve everyone in decisions about routines and choices and take cues from every family member. You're the parent and make the final decisions, but show your children you care by setting reasonable limits that include their participation.

🌸 **Create an environment that values learning.**
Continue to learn together in an environment where everyone becomes involved in the children's learning, which then encourages more learning.

🌸 **React well to successes and failures.**
Encourage family members to accept success humbly and failure with grace. Accept that you're all human and understand that nobody can be perfect, nor should you be.

🌸 **Show and say "I love you."**
The one common denominator of families that raise smart kids is their unconditional love for each other. Let your heart guide your parenting philosophy.

Ten Things to Do Every Day

❀ **Give hugs and kisses.**
Physical contact does a lot for humans. Holding, hugging, and giving gentle kisses help your children (and partner) in many ways.

❀ **Say, "Tell me more about that."**
Doing so helps your children express themselves more and lets you know more about what's going on in their world.

❀ **Tell your family members you love them.**
Even though you may show your love by the special things you do for your family, hearing the words "I love you" is also important.

❀ **Read to your kids.**
Doing so not only starts them down a good road toward loving books but also provides you with quiet time to be alone with them. Plus, kids who are read to (and who read) have higher IQs, better vocabularies, and increased language skills.

❀ **Validate your kids.**
Let your kids know that what they've just done or how they feel makes sense. Nothing is crueler than telling your kids that they're not feeling the way they say they're feeling — as in "Get up, you're not hurt!"

❀ **Feed your family nutritious foods.**
Make sure that your kids eat the right foods. Take care of yourself, too, to set a good example for your kids and to teach them about making better food decisions.

❀ **Talk to your kids.**
Every day you need to know what your kids are doing, where they've been, who they've been with, how they feel, and what their opinion is. Talking to your kids also starts a habit of open communication between you and your family.

❀ **Have a special time with each child.**
By spending time alone with your kids, making each child feel special and important, you help them not to feel lost in a large group; and, as a result, they feel more like a member of a family.

❀ **Provide caring behavior.**
Do that special thing that's meaningful to the person on the receiving end. When your child says that he loves it when you put a surprise in his lunch box, for example, make an effort to do that!

❀ **Practice patience.**
Get plenty of sleep, eat right, listen carefully, find out what makes your kids do what they do, ask yourself why you're losing your patience (whenever you are), and recognize when kids merely are being kids. Don't place unrealistic expectations on your kids, and pick your fights well.

Index

☺ ☻ ☹ ☺ ☻ ☹ ☺ ☻ ☹ ☺ ☻ ☹ ☺ ☻ ☹ ☺ ☺ ☻ ☹ ☺

Index

continued

Index

heat protection, 140–141
heater, 161
heatstroke, 141
height
  chart, 46–48
  preschooler, 41
  school-age child, 44
  toddler, 40
Heimlich maneuver, 163
hitting, 104
hormones, 45, 46, 85
hot tub, 165
hot water, 38
household chores. *See* chores
hug, 168
humidifier, 144
hyperactivity, 54
hypoallergenic sunscreen, 139

☺ **I** ☺

ibuprofen, 143
ice pack, 143
ignoring child, 106
illness. *See also* doctor; health
  cold, 154
  daycare, 121
  overview, 152
  prevention guidelines, 138–139
  resources, 153
  secondhand smoke, 138, 166
  signs, 153–154
  sitter, 122, 123
IM. *See* instant messaging
imagination, 30
immunizations, 146–150
independence
  family bed, 62
  school-age child, 83
  teenager, 85
  toddler, 80, 81–82
infection, 154, 155, 165
injury. *See* accident prevention;
    burn injury; safety
insect bite, 144
instant messaging (IM), 85
Institute for Athletics and
    Education, 56
Internet use, 17
interview
  babysitter, 122, 124–126
  doctor, 156
invalidating a problem, 7, 168
itchy skin, 144

☺ **J** ☺

junk food, 51, 53

☺ **K** ☺

kidnapping, 159
kissing, 138, 168
kitchen safety, 161–162, 163

☺ **L** ☺

label, food, 51
language
  correct English, 11
  discipline guidelines, 92
  hearing loss, 151
  potty-training readiness, 67
  preschooler, 40
  sibling rivalry, 105
  toddler, 38, 39
large motor skills. *See* motor skills
laughter, 8
lawn mower, 164
learning, 167. *See also* school
lecturing, 92
license, childcare, 121, 122
lip balm, 143
listening. *See also* communication
  behavior management, 27
  benefits, 168
  versus hearing, 12
  importance, 12
  parent's role, 6–7
  sibling rivalry, 106
  teenager's emotional development, 86
living room safety, 161
lock, cabinet, 38, 161
loneliness, 99
lost child, 158
lotion, 144
love, 167, 168
Love, Patricia *(The Emotional Incest
    Syndrome, What to Do When a
    Parent's Love Rules Your Life)*, 7
lunch, 51

☺ **M** ☺

manipulating children, 25
manners. *See* good manners
matches, 159
math, 42, 56

173

☺ ☺ ☹ ☺ ☺ ☹ ☺ ☺ ☹ ☺ ☺ ☹ ☺ ☺ ☹ ☺ ☺ ☺ ☹ ☺

☺ ☺ ☹ ☺ ☺ ☹ ☺ ☺ ☹ ☺ ☺ ☹ ☺ ☺ ☹ ☺ ☺ ☹ ☺

Index